■ *Cecil C.* ■

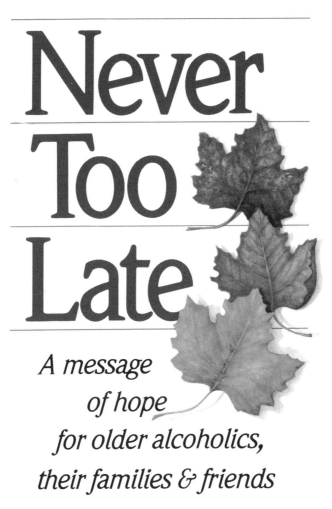

Never Too Late

*A message
of hope
for older alcoholics,
their families & friends*

■   ■   ■

CompCare®Publishers

2415 Annapolis Lane
Minneapolis, Minnesota 55441

© 1989 Cecil C.
All rights reserved.
Published in the United States
by CompCare Publishers.

C., Cecil.
     Never too late.

     1. Aged—Alcohol use.   2. Alcoholics—Treatment.
I. Title.
HV5138.C14   1989   362.2'928'0240565   89-1003
ISBN 0-89638-164-1

Cover design by Lillian Svec

Inquiries, orders, and catalog requests should be addressed to
CompCare Publishers
2415 Annapolis Lane
Minneapolis, Minnesota 55441
Call toll free 800/328-3330
(Minnesota residents 612/559-4800)

5	4	3	2	1
93	92	91	90	89

To the memory of Vesta

Contents

Foreword

This book is written to assist individuals in their understanding of alcoholism as it affects the elderly. It hopes to bring into perspective the obstacles and issues in identifying and treating elderly alcoholics. This population is the fastest growing group in America. As the number of elderly increases so does the public concern grow for the quality of life for this group. The essence of the message of this book is that: 1. Alcoholism is a disease. 2. The disease is treatable. 3. Resources are available. 4. Know them and use them. 5. The elderly alcoholic is not too old to be helped.

No better person is qualified to write about the elderly alcoholic than one who sobered up and began recovery at 70, Cecil C. His story appears in the story section of the "Big Book" of *Alcoholics Anonymous*, entitled "Those Golden Years." Cecil also has published many inspiring articles in AA's monthly magazine, the *A.A. Grapevine*. His experience in the alcoholism treatment field adds technical information about alcoholism among today's senior citizens. The author explores many myths and the stigma attached to the older alcoholic and the attitudes of the elderly that are possible barriers to recovery.

This book brings a message of hope to older drinkers and vital information to their concerned friends and loved ones. As Cecil observes, "Aging is a necessity, but maturity and recovery from alcoholism is a personal choice."

—Bill Pittman
President, Glen Abbey Books

1

Life Before Death

"Retirement must agree with you; you don't act like an eighty-nine-year-old man."

My friend, Dean, whom I had not seen in more than a decade, was sincere. I thanked him, adding, "Retirement nearly killed me during the first two years of my being *out to pasture*. Loneliness, boredom and a terrific consciousness of being totally unneeded overwhelmed me. Not having a job in which to bury myself anymore, I let the drink, which I had turned to in times of distress, take over. One day, after I was seventy, I woke up to the reality that I was an alcoholic."

He sucked in a breath. "Oh, no! I'm so sorry."

"Don't feel sorry. Call me *lucky*. I've had nineteen years of sobriety. This may be an old man's delusion, but I believe they have been the best years I've ever known."

I had been so artful at practicing hidden, solitary, dishonest drinking all my life that I had attained senior citizenry without ever losing any of the material things that drunks often forfeit. I explained that to Dean.

He frowned. "But, if you had drunk 'successfully' until you were past seventy, why in the world would you want to quit then?"

The answer was basically simple: I had become sick and tired of being sick and tired. When I retired at age sixty-eight, I looked forward to days of ease after more than forty years of steady, exciting, pressure work in public relations. But I began to discover that the days were becoming a drag. I had not done the "fine" writing I had planned. What I had finished, nobody wanted to publish. Who among still active friends wanted the company of an old man?

What did I have to look forward to? Increasing physical discomfort (although so far my illnesses had been minor), a build-up of loneliness and anger at a world that did not really need such accumulated wisdom as mine. I foresaw fewer and fewer creature comforts as inflation engulfed me while my retirement income remained stable. Alcohol was the only instrument of relief, even though on a temporary basis. With all my frustrations, it was reasonable, truly inevitable, I suppose, that my tippling would stop being fun and games.

I had been King Kong on roller skates during those years when I *lived to drink*. But I was among those "one out of ten" imbibers who, medical authorities tell us, will become alcoholics. Having crossed an invisible line into dependency, I arrived at the point where I had to *drink to live*.

Obsession marked the second stage of my drinking. Liquor had begun doing things *for* me, rather than *to* me. It filled an intense need. The alcohol which once gave me wings to fly now had taken away the sky. There was no place for lovely soaring.

There came for me, as there comes to most out-of-control alcoholics, that final, third stage of an addiction. *I drank to die.* That weird logic of an excessive drinker's fantasy told me I had lived too long. When one has ceased to be useful to anyone, including himself, it must be far too late to try to turn back. I was too old to hope for recovery, I thought.

Drinking oneself to death is not easy, but self-pity flourishes within the attempts to do so. One night in my bed, staring wide-eyed at a spinning ceiling, unable to touch a bursting head or quiet a hammering heart, I moaned out my despair: "With my rotten luck, I just might go on living in misery for another ten or more years."

For the first time in my life, I saw that I could forestall such a future by breaking free of the bottle. When I tried, I found I could quit drinking, sure. The problem was that I could not resist starting it all over again with still another "first drink." I was powerless . . . and frightened.

Human experience often reminds us that small miracles, revelations, and extraordinary awakenings can come to any person. One came to me within the darkness of my living room at three o'clock one morning, sitting in my favorite chair, shaking and sweating—and so God-awful alone. How I wanted another drink. But how well I knew the price I would pay.

As is the custom of one who drinks to die, I was thinking of the mysteries of death, appalled by that unanswerable question, "Is there life after death?" It is a thought that offers hope for the hopeless, help for the helpless and peace of mind for the depressed.

One moment of clarity descended to my troubled, confused mind. It was my own brief visit by a small miracle. "Life after death? Is that the point? Should it not be that my need is to know if there is life *before* death?"

I was simply going through daily agonized motions. Existing. Not really living.

That night, I reached my bottom, that low point in living beyond which I was fearful of sinking. Like all alcoholics, I had approached bottom repeatedly. But we addicted people can be champions at denying reality. Even old drunks have the ability to bounce back from jolting thuds and take refuge in the most readily available fantasy. Always, the result is another binge, another relapse, another painful fall.

That night, I realized that I was headed for either a hospital, a *funny farm* or death. If I continued to drink, I might live, but I would wish I had died.

If I were to save my life, there must be more of an awakening than hitting bottom. I would have to surrender. I must accept the necessity of smashing my grandiosity, stubbornness and sick ego. I had to replace them with humility. I saw that surrender is no more than confronting reality. Cold, harsh facts. The nobleness of truth in living. At that moment, I stopped playing God and began the process of finding a God.

Something I had once heard ran through my mind. *At any given moment, any person is the sum total of every choice he has made up to that time.*

Did I have one more choice? If so, it would not be to drink or not to drink. I had lost that choice. If I elected to woo alcohol again, I would surely be opting for death. I saw the one choice I just might have. To live or to die. I longed for one more chance at learning how to live *before* death.

Thank God, it was possible. But only because old attitudes can be replaced by healthy ones. Old dogs *can* learn new tricks. To reach for them, I first had to swallow the unhealthy pride that had continually sent me to the bottle for answers.

I had said I was lucky. Fortunately, I had several friends who were recovering alcoholics. I discovered that, even at the age of seventy, I could humbly ask for help and, more important, be grateful that help was generously, unselfishly available for the asking.

I had learned, early in life, to be a good listener. At fourteen years of age, I had started a newspaper career as a cub reporter on the *Emporia* (Kansas) *Gazette*. How attentive I was when editor William Allen White explained that all good reporters were careful listeners. He had emphasized the importance of paying attention to what others say. He said, "Remember, if God had intended that you talk more than listen, he'd have given you two mouths and only one ear." I remembered that as I began asking how I could preserve the sobriety I found when I began wanting it.

The most important of the initial advice I received was that I did not have the right to cry out, "Why me?" when misfortunes befell me, unless I used that same question—"Why me?"—when good fortune came into my life.

The day when my friend, Dean, had commiserated "I'm so sorry" about my alcoholism, I could accept his reaction to my open admission of my disease without dismay or rancor. I could understand his instinctive outcry. How could I expect him, a nonalcoholic, to relate to my own disease? Living with my arrested addiction, I had only a meager understanding of how a diabetic or an epileptic feels. Without personal identification, some mystery prevails. Of course, I regret society's misconception about problem drinking being a matter of character, weakness and morality. But I do not resent such unawareness.

As a volunteer with the National Council on Alcoholism (I was president for two years of a local chapter) I sometimes expressed discouragement at the slow progress toward eliminating the stigma of the disease. Then one day I savored the wisdom of a recovered woman alcoholic, who said, "I like to adopt the positive thinking of the experienced mountain climber who seldom looks upward to moan at the distance yet to be climbed, but turns to glance downward at the glorious vista emphasizing how very far he has come. We have indeed come a long way in the matter of education about alcoholism in only a few decades."

It was not really important that Dean understand my opinion that I was a lucky person. It was enough that *I* knew. The only tragedy I fear lies in my forgetting how incredible was this old drunk's change in attitude— something that has made it possible for me to experience life before death.

Why lucky? For one thing, my incurable disease does not demand incessant intake of medication or injections. It does not require a regime of harsh treatments. All I have to do is *not do something*. I just don't drink, no matter what provocation looms.

While alcoholism is not contagious, one factor of the disease *is* communicable. That is the joy we feel in attaining and maintaining sobriety.

I have discovered that, in arresting my obsessive dependency on alcohol, I have fortified and enriched my life. I know, too, that vigilance is essential to ensure my peace of mind. Otherwise, pressure-incubated depressions may slide me toward a relapse that could be fatal. And vigilance, once developed, is a top asset in our coping with modern living problems. I am grateful for it.

I recognize the difficulty we addicted people have in adjusting to a world where all people have problems because they are human. Troubles are the lot of all mankind. I am handicapped because years of experimenting with alcohol convinced me that the easiest, surest way out is through the use of such an artificial crutch as my favorite liquid drug. As a compulsive person it was normal for me to live under the influence of alcohol. Sobriety is unnatural. When I am denied a substance as important to my living patterns as alcohol was, a great void exists.

What filled that gap in my life was personal growth along new paths. The most accessible road to that growth is a *way* called involvement. *Action* in working a recovery program is the magic word for me. Through meaningful involvement with others, I've achieved at least a modicum of serenity. A young man once described to me the perfect illusion of serenity as being a majestic swan gliding over the placid waters of a lake. Yet, unseen in this serene picture are two sturdy legs beneath the surface, making powerful strokes so that the serene bird can progress toward a goal.

Giving of myself requires constant attention to shedding the emotional immaturity that made me dependent on alcohol. I must remember that aging is a necessity but maturity is a personal choice. I'd grown old beyond my years while drinking. But in seeking life before death, I found a youthful way of thinking.

My totally enjoyable "pre-death" life today depends wholly on my altered attitudes. I have taken firm steps toward moderation in all things. My character defects and shortcomings have been cut down in size and I can live with them. I have learned to use my emotions positively, trying to maintain a proper balance between those that bring me joy and the ones that can be detrimental. I know now that emotions are human; only robots are without them. All emotion, bad or good, spells energy. To live fully, we need controlled zest and vitality from every source. In order to grow, I had to learn to like myself, rather than being my own worst enemy.

It is surprising how teachable we can be once we invite humility and gratitude into our minds. During the first year of my growth in sobriety, I had a solid lesson in the difference between accepting my lot and being resigned to its reality.

As a retiree on a fixed income, I am one of millions who find economics hard to take. How few are the theater tickets, the "resort" outings and the fine restaurant dinners for my wife and me. I was feeling sorry for myself as a captive of soaring taxes and insurance rates—and the cost of staples. Why should one who had worked hard for nearly a half century and tasted good things as a movie studio executive be reduced to tight squeezing of small coins?

Then, as a "veteran" of one year without a drink, I visited a friend I had made in the movie business. Fifteen years younger than I, he had been a Big Man on Campus at the university where I earned my degree. I had helped him several times. We were friends, but of different worlds. He was incredibly wealthy.

But now he, too, was an alcoholic. He lived alone, unable to work. Emaciated beyond belief, bloated of liver, haggard. Yet cleaned and cared for by servants. His wife was long gone with his children. He was friendless.

I sat beside his silk-sheeted bed, drinking coffee tapped from a sterling silver urn by a manservant while he drank the martinis that were his medication. He lay, unable to get drunk or to become sober. And we talked. Mostly of my recovery, because he had asked me to come there and tell him about it.

Suddenly, he said, "My God, how much I want what you have." He had everything I had regretted not having. Except for sobriety. Of that, he did not have what he must have seen glowing within me.

I was thrilled that he *did* want it. I got him to a hospital. But, as it luckily had not been for me, it was too late for him. He died there, alone amid affluence.

And my self-pity went away when I recalled what he had said and when I suddenly remembered an experience told me by a woman named Dorothy. Her home had been burglarized. Many fancy baubles and beloved keepsakes had been stolen. The more she looked, the more she found missing—and the more her sense of loss grew until she was in tears.

"Suddenly, I returned to sanity," she told me. "I asked what of great, lasting and meaningful importance had been stolen? And I knew that nobody can ever rob me of the important things in my life—my sobriety, self-respect, peace of mind, the love of family and friends, the ability to share precious thoughts, the capacity for spiritual, emotional and physical growth. All the things I had built out of the wreckage of my past. I knew that nobody but myself ever could take from me the greatest things in life."

So I appreciate the good things I do have—my home, family and all that Dorothy mentioned. And I understood why my dying alcoholic acquaintance would want something that I had.

I have them today because life has permitted me a chance to grow. To grow, I must first know myself; until I am fully aware of the drawbacks that fetter me, I cannot work to reduce them. Even knowing is not enough. I must create a willingness to grow. Before we want to be better, we have to want to want. I know that my growth is not a destination. Growing is a happy journey. It preserves my chances of living before death.

Life gives me simple goals. I strive, each day, to be the best me I've ever been. A recovering alcoholic of twenty gave me that symbol of spiritual growth. Surely, if on any day, I am not worse than yesterday, I am holding my own. I am not retrogressing. I recognize that constant victory is not possible. No man can be perfect. How dull it would be if we were.

My favorite word now is serendipity. Unanticipated blessings have been many for me. I am thankful that my recovery from alcoholism forces me to handle my emotions and suppress character defects. Victims of other diseases may try to be *nicer* persons simply to live more comfortably. My addiction says that if I don't think and behave more positively, I am in danger of experiencing a relapse that could lead to death.

It was a major character change when I was able to ask for help from others. As the oldest of three brothers, I had taken over the handling of family problems when they emerged. I had been a dedicated achiever and an avowed people-pleaser. To get places, I had always made "I Did It My Way" my theme song. My motto had been: never ask favors from anyone. Anything worth doing was worth doing to excess.

Serendipity must have filled the air the day I broke down and held out empty hands and an emptier heart. I never dreamed that the tools given me to sober up and live comfortably in total abstinence are the same tools needed to become a better person.

Of all the tools for character growth, the most useful ones for me have been love, honesty and sharing. I have found that I can dispel rancor and resentment by deliberately extending love to those whom I consider unlovable; ultimately, in my mind at least, they become lovable.

Honesty has many helping hands but I could not grasp any of them until I understood that I could not be honest with the world until I developed self-honesty. For this crotchety, selfish old man to eagerly engage in acts of service and giving, I had to seek a 180-degree change. Out of my altered attitudes came a sense of being needed. When I was able to do a good deed without anyone else knowing about it, that was really a hallmark in spiritual growth.

My most rewarding daily effort is taking inventories of my emotions. Each time I examine and correct a troublesome emotion or fortify one that shows weakness, growth is inevitable. To cope in a *now* world, we must make constructive approaches toward adapting the feelings by which we live.

It was an unexpected revelation that, in character growth as in maintaining sobriety, I could expect myself to do so only to the best of my ability. My recovering friends say, "It takes what it takes" and "Different strokes for different folks." I am not in a recovery program because of how someone else drank. Only as a result of my own guzzling. Nor can I change myself on the basis of how my best friend misbehaved. Each person is his or her own lifelong assignment. Whatever progress I make must be sufficient in my mind. To want more than I am capable of reaping for myself can lead to feelings of rejection, inadequacy and failure.

The need to grow has taught me that no person is too old to look for life before death. It is rarely too late for attitudes to be altered. While we are wisely advised that *easy does it*, if we are to avoid devastating impatience, we still *must do it*. I was reminded early in my recovery that if I wish to go from Los Angeles to New York, I first must leave Los Angeles. To give up old ideas and outmoded patterns of living is not just desirable. It's a must.

In working on becoming a "better me," I am constantly reminded that my past is only for visiting briefly in order to recall what it was like. I must not live there. The future can only begin with each moment in which I live, since today truly is the first day of the rest of my life. I have the power to make it the best.

As a problem drinker, I applauded the cynicism that "faith is the utter rejection of reality." Now I covet faith. Reality reminds me that despair is the absence of faith. If I am to know life before death I must live with faith.

And so I have tried to live for the past nineteen years that have been filled with a peace of mind, acceptance and love for my fellow man since the night of November 22, 1969, when, at seventy years of age, I walked shakily into my first Alcoholics Anonymous meeting.

For the past nineteen years, I have tried to live with faith. Heeding the often-quoted fact that "Faith without works is dead," I must continue to practice what I'm told and study and read about my disease.

I have learned that abstinence can produce the proper soil for a garden that will, for all who plant well and attend to the growth of maturing, produce not only *life before death* but a fuller life in added years of a newly found way of living free.

Because I surrendered to reality on November 22, 1969, at the age of seventy, and chose to seek a joyful and pleasurable sobriety, I have learned that at any time during my "old age" I can improve my understanding of acceptance, peace of mind, honesty, gratitude, humility and, above all, a love that has no limitations in giving and receiving.

I have learned these pleasures of sober character growth, and much more, because the well to which I went to quench the thirst for the happier way to live was the fellowship of Alcoholics Anonymous.

2

Welcome to a New World

At the second meeting of recovering alcoholics which I attended, shyly and perhaps pathetically, I was greeted by a husky-voiced middle-aged man with a face that never discarded its smile. I told him that I was emotionally unsure of myself because I was brand new among problem drinkers in search of sobriety.

His hand met mine. "Welcome to a new world," he said. And in Alcoholics Anonymous this old man found a new world.

How understandable it is that living without liquor for a senior citizen who had been drinking to die can mean a whole new world. Entrance into a life refreshingly and rewardingly different from old patterns, however, is not a privilege exclusively for the elderly. A new world assuredly beckons to anyone who makes a character change, or who works to free himself from any major addiction or minor dependency. It is available to those who wish to live with less tension from compulsions and excessiveness. Altered attitudes come with the awareness of a Higher Power to which a person can turn over the problems of coping in society until spiritual guidance gives him or her the solution.

It just happens that the unwelcome monkey on my back was the ever-progressive and ultimately fatal disease of alcoholism.

During the early months of my life in the new world of sobriety, I would explain, with sincerity, that I had been motivated toward it by a series of incredible coincidences. It is a fact that an addicted person's awakening to facets of reality often is a slow process. So I do not regret that I went on uttering that bit of debatable wisdom for a couple of years before a remark by a friendly woman opened a closed door of my mind that was keeping out much more of value than it was locking inside.

Her smile was broad when she asked, "Did you ever pause to realize that a coincidence is only a miracle for which God chooses to remain anonymous?"

That remark prompted a spiritual conversation for this old man who had long been a nonbeliever. I had spent five years getting my college A.B. (B.A.) degree because wanderings into scientific subjects of all kinds deferred accumulated credits toward my "major."

I was convinced that cosmic science and the evolution of species accounted for everything that "less intellectual" persons believed were the results of spiritual blessings. Self-professed atheists recognize the infallibility of mathematics in the order of physical existence.

So it was a minor shock to find that the woman's advice was shaking my agnosticism. A "scientific thinker" has to rely on the absolute credibility of the law of averages. And these laws did not make reasonable the number of unusual events that lumped themselves into the rapid succession of *happenstances* and *accidents* that made me do something about my desire to quit drinking.

The day I quit utilizing rationalization to supply me with excuses and alibis, I realized that each man, in his own way, has access to a power greater than himself. It warmed me to know that trust and faith in such a potential for solutions could minimize threats to my peace of mind and security.

Without the confidence that some kind of guidance can be derived from conscious or unconscious prayer, the feelings of rejection, inadequacy and not being needed by society would create depression. And the PLOMs (Poor Little Old Me) of self-pity are a short step away from a relapse in vigilance. If I get drunk again, I'll surely die.

I am sure that even the arrogant can grow to admire some of the simple truths with which my world abounds. Once, I would have called most philosophy corny and banal.

The mind of the addicted person seems to be an open receptacle in which to file pertinent truths that at first fly over the head of the listener with a "what was that?" reaction. When the advice is voiced later, the meaning gets through. That, I am sure, is why in recovery groups of addicted men and women, repetition is not avoided. The world calls it "sinking in," of course. We alcoholics frequently come to a sudden identification with a remark we are *hearing* for the first time although it has flown past us on dozens of previous occasions.

So, as the date of my last drink got further and further into the past, my world revealed a bountiful crop of useful messages that an unfogged brain began to recall. In a way, I was grateful that my brain was temporarily gin-soaked while I first tried to listen. When my mind, after clearing, grasped twice-told tales, the truths made deep impressions.

For example, I was hearing well when someone told me that it requires charity to forgive others, but wisdom to forgive myself.

The word *love* once was banal, inane and almost repugnant to this veteran of four decades in the cutthroat realm of movie press agentry. But I nodded when I heard that love is no more than wishing someone well. Thus, I could love someone without ever liking him.

In the sharing of an addiction and a common solution for arresting it, we naturally can wish no one anything greater than continued sobriety. This being true, I was told we could not criticize those who had relapses and drank again. Perhaps it was a matter of "there but by the grace of God, go I."

It is not possible to look with disdain on those who return after a drunken binge that has broken a record of sobriety. I was reminded of the story of a crippled child who had fallen while trying to walk. When she had dried her tears and gotten to her feet again, she was told there is no disgrace in falling down in any endeavor. The only shame lies in not trying again. . .and again. . . .

As a friend likes to say, "Live in my heart and pay no rent."

As a senior citizen, it was good to hear that I must enjoy aging, since it is a privilege sadly denied many.

When I approached arrogance, I was reminded that arrogant people may often be wrong but are never in doubt. And humility was gently thrust at me when my visions of sainthood became obvious; someone was sure to remind me how easy it is to mistake senility for serenity. Humility, by the way, was explained to me as a self-induced state of being teachable.

Because alcoholism is a disease that constantly tries to tell any victim that he doesn't have it, I must remain mindful that alcoholism is incurable. I know I will die an alcoholic; will I die sober? I understood the truth that all imbibers eventually take that last drink, but we who recover are people who have lived to talk about that last drink.

I will never wander from the help of others if I remember that addicted people are people who need people. Nobody can recover for me, yet I can't do it alone. How true the remark: "We can do what I can't."

Before I could remember and react to these and other "adages," I had to open my mind through an act of surrender to reality. I could not explain my decision to stop drinking by saying that a string of happenstances had shaken me up. They had, however, combined to make it clear to even a sick mind that "something surely is trying to tell me something."

My chain of coincidences started in Tucson, Arizona, where I finished a small chore around Easter time, 1969. I got disgracefully drunk at a house party on Saturday evening. I awoke the next morning knowing that an old Los Angeles drinking buddy named Verne, now living in Arizona and whom I had not seen for ten years, was picking me up just before noon. I looked forward to subduing my hangover with bits of the dog that bit me that Verne would supply.

As a gesture, I telephoned the hostess of the preceding night's party and apologized for my behavior. "But I want you to know that I've just called Alcoholics Anonymous and they're sending someone to straighten me out." I laughed. She didn't laugh.

Verne arrived, took one look at me and launched into a personal story of how he had gone to the bottom of the living barrel with booze seven years before and had gone to A. A. and been sober ever since. Another coincidence? He detailed all the symptoms and ravages of alcoholism and described the joys of recovery. To show him I had no problem, I turned down a drink before Easter dinner.

Back home, I encountered another coincidence when I misread an address one fumbling afternoon and wound up at a desk where a young woman asked, "May I help you?" I said I really didn't know.

"This is the Alcoholism Council, you know."

I didn't know. I said so and made a quick exit. Things were getting a little sticky.

A week or so later, they got even heavier. Intoxicated but reasonably alert, I was watching late-late TV when, at station break, a public service spot flashed on. "If you have a drinking problem," said voice and title. The place to contact was the Alcoholism Council. I quickly switched channels.

Ironically, the same damned blurb appeared on that second channel. It was a coincidence that rattled my teeth.

I always sat in my big red leather chair late at night trying to quiet the shakes while I thought about things that might have been different. One night, I recalled a scene in *Shane*, a film I had publicized during my press agent days. I always liked that line from Alan Ladd to a grizzly villain: "The problem with you, old man, is that you've lived too long."

I identified with that dialogue. "That's my line," I muttered. "The story of my sad ending. I've drunk too long and I'm of no use to anyone. It's a good thing I'm drinking myself to death."

A few nights later, I was in the depths of self-pity and defeatism when a frightening thought came. Supposing I did not die soon? What if I had to go on hurting from too much booze for another ten or fifteen years? The idea was harrowing. But alas, not a sobering thought. I kept on swigging.

Almost abruptly, it seemed that the media was conniving to frighten me. TV fiction began to relate too many stories about drunks. Newspapers and magazines appeared to be concentrating on soul-shaking discoveries about people who drink to excess. The crazy thing was that I eagerly read them all when nobody was noting my interest in the subject. When alone, I'd watch those *sad* TV episodes. I was not about to make it an open secret that the subject was getting to me. So I gulped liquor to prove to them, and to myself, that I was physically and mentally immune.

One day in the dentist's office I picked up a magazine I never would have opened by personal choice. And I read a little from an article about something in which I hadn't an iota of interest—reincarnation.

A boxed headline was meant to attract attention. It got mine. It asked why a soul should not come back in a new body.

I naturally pondered that one a bit. What if I came back the same old me? Suppose I returned as another helpless alcoholic? I'd have this suffering to do all over again, from start to finish. And, my God, what if there was no alcohol for those born with what my Irish friends call *a strong weakness*?

I concluded that maybe I ought to solve my problem in this lifetime. It was a deep concern. Not, however, impelling enough to make me put the plug in the jug yet.

The week of November 12 through November 22 brought an increase in the number, frequency and unusualness of my incredible coincidences. Those last seven days of my drinking started with an episode early Monday afternoon when I was drinking alone while my wife was at a club luncheon.

My cup ran dry and I got up to tap my hidden supply. My rise was too sudden. I wobbled a bit, listed to the right, veered more sharply and lost my ability to stand upright. I fell against the lower part of the room's wall. An object fell onto my head.

I got to my knees and first looked for the glass I'd dropped. Then I saw that I had been konked by a plaque which had been given me only a few months earlier at the awards luncheon of the Hollywood Publicists Guild, a group for whom I had been an early president. The award had been a special recognition for distinguished service.

The dignity of a white-haired *elder statesman* sure as hell slipped a long way that day. A simple object—an uncorked booze bottle—had kicked the props from under me. It was time for me to admit that I had lost all power over alcohol. It was time, yes, but I didn't leap at the conclusion. My ego had more to say about running my life, wrecked as it was.

Two nights later, while my wife slept soundly, I decided that it would be bad for my lifetime image if, after I'd secretly drunk myself to death, someone found that cache of empties I had been filing in a big storage space high in the kitchen. I judged that I was sober enough to climb onto a chair and carefully clean out that army of "dead soldiers."

A moment of sudden body weaving as I stood on the chair made me doubt my steadiness. But the wobbling stopped. As I worked at gathering the souvenirs of my recent drinking days, I sensed the presence of an observer. I turned to see my wife staring with dismay and a touch of horror. She had not dreamed that I had been consuming so much grog.

Later, I learned that we had experienced another small, sharp California earthquake. It had awakened her.

Alcoholics are opportunists. I stepped down from the chair, took her by the arm and said, "Come. I want to talk with you about all those bottles."

We sat on the sofa and I told her things I never realized I knew about myself. I said I was an alcoholic and had an incurable disease. It could be arrested. All I had to do was get physically free of the beatings from alcohol. I could find help in handling the addiction and obsession. I knew where to go and, if she just stayed calm, I'd get at it tomorrow—or the day after. I told her that I would seek help in A.A. I knew it would work!

I began relating all the things Verne had told me and which I had tried not to let sink in. And I was relating to Verne's former problems, too.

Of course I did not go to A.A. for help the next day. Nor the next. But I did feel the jolt of delayed reaction on Saturday night of that week. That afternoon, television carried the biggest football game of the season in Los Angeles, USC against UCLA, with the Rose Bowl at stake. It was exciting. Every senior citizen knows that too much excitement can be fatal. Most drunks are aware that booze is a depressant and curbs overnervousness. So I drank, matching my adrenaline flow against Vodka's soporific effects. I passed out just as the game ended.

I came to lying on the divan. The TV was off. It looked like dinner was over and dishes washed. Had I helped with preparation and clean up? Had I even eaten? The utter confusion shocked me. I felt guilty. I had not kept my promise to my wife—and myself. Real shame arose.

Guilt and shame motivated me across the room to the telephone. I found in the directory the number for the closest clubhouse where A.A. meetings took place.

I dialed the number. At that moment, a miracle occurred. All the coincidences began motivating my life. It wasn't until many months later that I realized that coincidences are indeed small miracles, the result of prayer—even silent prayer, or those miserable words I cried out so often, late at night: "God help me."

As I have progressed spiritually in Alcoholics Anonymous with wise and caring people, I have come to understand what truly had transpired in my tired, confused old mind that night. The first step in A.A. can be taken without an alcoholic realizing it. So it was that on an evening shortly before November 22, when I told my patient, suffering wife that I was an alcoholic, I had surrendered. I admitted my powerlessness over alcohol to a single person.

What I later found to be true was that first promises can be readily forgotten or postponed under the spell of denial. My ego, savoring the taste of grandiosity, told me I could do it my way and that I must not make new commitments quickly. I had not yet learned patience. Old ideas persisted and took the forms of cop-outs, excuses, alibis, sneaky action and stubborn refusals to believe I needed help.

But all the denial left me momentarily when I came to in my big red leather chair full of shame, guilt and self-pity, crying out for help. I was ready to humbly, gratefully and honestly accept the help that I knew could save an old man's life.

Although I still was in a state of alcoholic confusion, my surrender was enough to begin restoring me to the sanity that is reality.

The ego that nourishes denial was, incredibly, to urge me to retreat and "take back my surrender" several times that evening before I was in a position to receive a "message."

I had only one thing going for me that night. I had belief. It was the belief which prompts faith and trust in the power of A.A. I had seen the program work with others. I had never asked A.A. for help but close friends of mine had and they had been sober from the moment of their surrender. I knew I could call them but I also knew I could go quickly on my own to the fellowship where they had found lasting sobriety. There had been seven of them, five fellow publicists and newsmen. And two actor friends. One actor later became my sponsor. The other was a founder of A.A. in the Los Angeles area and died sober a few years ago.

I have come to be proud and grateful for the faith which my ego tried to shake but failed to do. I had belief, not only in the miracle of A.A.'s principles, but in the surety that all I had to do was ask sober men and women for guidance.

I am sure, today, that one cannot experience a miracle unless he believes miracles will guide him to serenity and security. So I walked with a belief that engendered faith. Later, I would hear and read many times that "Faith without acts is dead" and I was to accept the truth that faith will become strangled if we do not begin to share, to be involved with others and to learn to love.

Little of this was giving me the trust I needed so badly or an understanding of where I was going that evening. And in my carrying out my decision, I kept fighting off the near-success of denial.

So I dialed the A.A. number and waited. For a moment only. I often have wondered where fate may have taken me if no one had answered. But there was an answer.

A feminine voice said, "A.A."

I asked, "Is there a meeting tonight?"

"We have a meeting here every night of the year."

"What time?"

"Eight-thirty."

"Eight-thirty? Okay, honey, I'll be there."

Why was I so friendly and familiar? Perhaps, the sound of a voice, thick with love, not booze.

Then I looked at the clock and denial returned with an excuse. It was 8:25. A grandiose ego told me I'd missed out. I could never get there in time to receive any help. So I'd skip it until later. Later? Tomorrow was Sunday. "There wouldn't be a meeting on Sunday," I decided. "That's not a church."

But the miracle business was still working. My lovely wife stood in the doorway from the bedroom. She had been on the bed reading the paper and, by chance, had picked up the telephone. Probably to inform our daughter, "Pop's that way again."

The question she asked deflated my denial. "Who was the honey I just heard you making a date with for 8:30 tonight?"

At the age of seventy, I should have been flattered at her intimation that I still was capable of a touch of romance.

But the thought that she still was unsure of my faithfulness made me defensive. "That was A.A. and I'm going there tonight and you can't stop me."

"It's about time," was her reply.

So I threw water on my face and used a towel and comb and, when I was out of the bathroom, she had her coat on and held the car keys.

She said she was driving me to our daughter's house, on the way to the clubhouse, and wanted our daughter to get me to the meeting. When I replied I was capable of finding the place, she replied, "I think not. Wouldn't it be ironic for you to get a drunk-driving ticket on your way to your first A.A. meeting?"

I was on my way to where my surrender meant me to be. But old Denying Ego still made a try. As my wife prepared to get out of the car and go in to stay with our grandchildren while our daughter got me to where sobriety was dispensed, I held on to her arm.

"Let's not be too hasty," I cautioned.

"I thought you'd given up all that nonsense."

My ego made one last-ditch try. "I hate being embarrassed and I know I will be if I try to get into that meeting. I know that A.A. is a religious organization and there will be someone dressed in white standing in the door and they'll refuse to let me in unless I assure them that I believe in God. And I'm an agnostic."

She had never heard that excuse before. So I began the last leg of a short trip to my first A.A. meeting.

We arrived late. And, behold, there was someone in white in the doorway and I whispered, "Wow. It's true." But he was waiting for someone and only said, "Hi."

My daughter and I entered the club. The meeting was well in progress. Spirits were high and voices alive with laughter and the exchange of happy words.

It was "Young People's Night" at the club.

My persistent denying ego told me I had an excuse to leave. I was among children. No way! I told my daughter, "I'm getting out."

But the magic of sobriety miracles was still at work.

A middle-aged man had overheard me. It was an open meeting and, although only the young participated, people of any age would be welcomed. Even an old man like me, I found.

He introduced himself as Frank and asked, "Where are you going?"

"Out," I informed him. "I'm leaving. I'm in the wrong place."

"From the way you look and smell, I'd say you are in the right place."

"A.A., yes. But not a children's meeting. I'm seventy. You tell me how I can identify with a roomful of children?"

"Easy. Just sit down and listen. I'm sure you'll discover there's no generation gap in A.A.—or anywhere in recovery."

How right he was. I sat and listened. I saw a sign, "We Care," on the wall above a podium and I remembered how many nights I had sat alone in my red chair, moaning "Nobody cares."

And I saw another sign. "Keep Coming Back." I thought about how often some hostess had refrained, at the end of a party, from asking me to ever come back again.

And I identified with the leader of that meeting. She was only fourteen and I was seventy but something told me that if I got sober and she stayed abstinent, I'd have as much chance of making the program as she had. But if I went back into the cold of drunkenness and she slipped back into a life of drinking, that fourteen-year-old girl would have as much chance of dying from alcoholism as this old man had.

The only sharing I remembered was the most important thing I heard that evening. A young man named Jim, age nineteen, who had been sober one year and one week, spoke briefly from the podium and glowingly reported, "Today, because of A.A. I sincerely believe that I am the best me I've ever been."

And I told myself, "Old man, you are the worst you've ever been. It's about time you heeded what comes out of the mouths of babes."

I began to smile and to glow and to relate to those happy "children" who were so grateful for sobriety that it filled the whole room.

I have not had a drink since that night.

I knew, even before being told when I came back the second time, that I was in a new world and was welcome to partake of the good things it offered.

3

The World I Left

It is natural to suppose that any alcoholic who reaches the age of seventy before choosing to try for sobriety must have severely damaged such vital organs as the liver, heart, brain, kidney, bladder, stomach and, for men, the precious prostate gland.

However, it was my good fortune that a human's tolerance for alcohol begins to decrease the moment he or she is born. Intolerance at sixty for even a first drink is devastatingly greater than at twenty.

It is, therefore, understandable that my addiction was expedited the moment I began to concentrate on boozing for my own "comfort" as I approached retirement age. Until I began "letting down the bars," I had drunk cautiously. I was expertly trained not to drink while working. A business lunch or dinner was "on the job." I watched clients get sloshed while I stayed craftily capable of host duties. Any "satisfying" imbibing was done secretly and alone.

My pattern of serious ingestion of liquor was established between the time I was ousted from a spot as publicity director at a major studio at age sixty and my retirement at sixty-eight. I remained steadily on salary at various studios and agencies while my capitulation to alcohol slowly developed. Liquor never interferred dramatically with my professional and family life on my way to retirement. Sly, sneaky, deceitful drinking was my forte.

I had set myself up for a drastic change in drinking patterns by the time I became a pensioner. My body and its organs had become excessively susceptible to the effects from any day's first drink.

I was slow to learn that unless man profits by his mistakes, he is doomed to continue repeating them for the remainder of his life. Whenever I tried serious sharing in social drinking, I lapsed into the dullness of passing out all too quickly. The resulting feelings of rejection and inadequacy and of guilt, remorse and humiliation did not, however, prod me toward trying to stay sober. My behavior only created a caution about "partying" alcoholically with practically everyone else. I became a *loner*.

Because I entered the world of solitary drinking at a time when my tolerance was at ebb tide, the progression of alcoholism took off like a one-hundred-meter sprinter. My emotional stability collapsed before alcohol could destroy my body.

My recovery among alcoholics of all shapes and sizes taught me the futility of asking, "Why did this happen to me?" There could never be a definitive answer. No alcoholic can know why he is among those one-in-ten drinkers who cross the invisible line into an addiction while the other nine escape.

To ask "why?" is to look for excuses, reasons, cop-outs. Such askers merely are seeking someone or something to blame. One of my friends terms alibi-searchers "blame throwers."

I had to learn that, rather than asking "Why?", I should inquire, "What am I going to do about the problem?"

Why I was a late starter in the art of "gracious drinking" is of little importance. Actually, I grew up fearing liquor. I had much pity and more intolerance for those men (my God, no *lady* ever got tipsy) who became intoxicated. My hometown, Emporia, was one of the most arid of the dry spots in bone-dry Kansas. The Volstead Act that created prohibition meant little to us Jayhawkers. The sale of alcoholic beverages had been unlawful for generations before mine.

There was a sad old joke about the farmer who named his cow "Kansas" because the animal had been dry for so long. Those of us who imitated city slickers downed bottles of near beer (entirely nonalcoholic), which was commonly referred to as "belly wash."

I was too busy being a big young frog in my little hometown and later in Los Angeles, pressing constantly at being a Big Man On Campus until graduation from USC, to experiment with booze. Even when I concentrated on beginning a career and a married life, I would not have guzzled had I been able to find and afford bootleg. There were too many believable horror stories about poor imbibers going blind from a gulp of the bad stuff.

With much naivete, I reached the age of thirty-two before I had my first drink, and simultaneously my first drunk. The episode probably contributed nothing toward my developing alcoholism more than a third of a century later. But it did determine an attitude toward public drinking that I pursued all my life.

I was a veteran of four years in movie publicity when I had my first adventure in drinking intoxicants. An artful people-pleaser all my life, I took pride in currying the favor of bosses and celebrities to whom I gave my attention. I connived for "plum" assignments.

Looking back from retirement, I realize that I always managed to get myself attached to colorful stars on films that had the "chemistry" to entice big media coverage. It happened with Clara Bow, W. C. Fields, the Marx Brothers, Maurice Chevalier, George M. Cohan, Earl Carroll, Gary Cooper, Carole Lombard, Tallulah Bankhead, Charles Laughton and Bing Crosby, among others. At the sunrise of the thirties, a comedy team named Moran and Mack became a natural sensation through a recording, "The Two Black Cows." These blackfaced comics, sophisticated in show business through vaudeville, Broadway and radio, signed a two-picture deal with Paramount. I wanted to work with them, to learn another road to fame and fortune. I managed to handle both of their films.

During the first, *Why Bring That Up?*, Charley Mack, who owned the act with Moran (real name Searcy) working for him, hosted a Halloween party at a mansion he and his wife had leased in Beverly Hills. He asked my boss to let me invite and keep happy some important press people with whom Mack was anxious to become palsy.

I attended with my young wife and a studio photographer. There was a bar and an expert to whip up fancy drinks. I was anxious to impress Mack and his guest notables and to cope at libation with the liquor-knowledgeable members of the media. As each newsperson requested a favorite (and different) combination, I was impelled to match his intake and have "one of the same." I was the only person at the party to get drunk. I because sick and barely managed to get to the master bathroom upstairs before eruption. My poor wife had to clean up while I lay in disgrace, remorse and guilt on a silken bedspread.

Embarrassment was a haunting sensation for months to come. I was sure every person I approached in the industry had heard about my disgrace and was secretly chortling amid disdain and pity. My boss scornfully explained to me that press agents never got drunk while working. I had been "on the job." It was never to happen again. It never did. I vowed then that nobody who counted in my scheme of attracting approval would ever again see me so weak-willed.

It was a natural stage-setting for my future design for drinking—vigilant deceit and connivance. I ultimately became an artful dodger, a cover-upper, a hider of bottles, a denier of excessive intakes and a consumer in self-elected solitude. I was to identify later when I heard a definition of an alcoholic as a person who stops bragging about drinking and starts lying about it.

As a dedicated people-pleaser working toward an addiction, I became so expert at keeping my drinking behavior secret that I easily created an image of professional reliability and social uprightness that fooled all but my suffering wife and family.

After I admitted my alcoholism and began abstinence, I was never surprised when friends, upon being told about my battle with booze, were amazed, disbelieving and sometimes shocked. I already had proof that I had fooled close acquaintances. Once, while driving a friend back to a place which I learned was a recovery house for alcoholics, I told him, "I think I'm an alcoholic, too." He laughed, shook his head and said, "No way. You're not the type."

All of the significant symptoms of an impending dependency have come back to my more stable mind after sobriety was attained. Recently, I had another reminder of my old world. I had been asked, through my involvement with the Alcoholism Council's program, to speak to a class of graduate students at the Univeristy of Southern California. I lunched on the campus with a friend who felt impelled to take me to the office of the university daily, *The Trojan*, and introduce me as editor of the paper in 1923–24. The result was an interview. When the story appeared, I was alerted to one of my statements, printed in the box, boldly presented in ten-point type.

It was a comment about my forty years as a movie press agent. The words flashed: "Hollywood was a rat race. Working with stars and temperamental directors, you have to become a terrible people-pleaser. It would be okay if you liked the people, but I don't remember really liking any of the people I had to please."

Reading that, my wife gulped. "I don't think I'd have said that," she commented. My words rang with nastiness. I did have regrets at having voiced such a feeling. But no remorse. Guilt seldom rides in the saddle with reality. Instead of dwelling on "if only I hadn't" aspects of an inadvertent openness about an unpleasant fact, I asked myself why it was true.

Not liking any of the people whose approval I eternally sought and whom I hoped to impress was *my* fault, not theirs. Of course, there are pompous bores and arrogant egomaniacs and downright mean persons among celebrities. I once expressed the opinion that I had observed that no person ever could succeed without being totally selfish.

Of course, among all those whom I had enjoyed knowing, a large number were worthy of being liked. It was my choice to like few of them. A lifetime spent in pleasing people equipped me with a resistance to opening myself up to deep hurt feelings if a personality should expose me to rejection and a feeling of inadequacy.

Anyone with that kind of an attitude is a prime target for disillusionment when unavoidable rejections and examples of Hollywood's caste system befall him. This is the common fate of all people-pleasers, and I was an approval-seeker from childhood.

A people-pleaser invariably starts out being naive. It is, therefore, a rude awakening, often resulting from an incredibly long period of experiencing rebuffs, when one learns that many people cannot or will not be charmed by "achievers."

My drive to induce others to like me was prompted by the ever-present feeling that although I was born on the right side of the tracks, I actually belonged on the wrong side. When I rubbed elbows with important and affluent people and often partook of the best material things in life, in my heart I always *knew* that I neither belonged nor deserved.

The successes I experienced from my people-pleasing did nothing to give me the humility that I needed so badly once I started on the road of recovery. Hence, my greatest rapid character growth in those early weeks of recovery was in humility, since I started with so little.

We in recovery from alcoholism incessantly laugh over how little we deceived the rest of the world with our sneakiness. We often were the *last* to know we had a drinking problem. So, I must suspect that some persons saw through my act. One who did was my French teacher at college, a Miss Saby. One day, she detained me after class and put on a friendly smile to show that she meant to be helpful.

"Someday, somewhere, you are going to face up to a situation where your charm act is not going to help you get by. I hope it won't be too much of a blow to your pride. But it will come. Why don't you start now trying to utilize your talents instead of relying on pleasing everybody with so little meaningful effort?''

Her talk was long remembered, but long unheeded. Since she gave me an A in class, I figured that I really could fool all of the people all of the time.

When, at the age of sixty, I lost the best job I ever had, I shrugged and called it, "The way the ball bounces." I was so sure that the opinion in my profession was that "everybody likes him." I had never stood in the unemployment line. I had been president of my Guild, recipient of a "man of the year" award, a governor of the Academy, and chairman of the Publicity Directors' Committee, and I was engaged in a lot of activity aimed at making me "a credit to the industry."

I continued to please people and benefit from the image that remained untarnished. I was a lone drunk because old souses cannot influence people if their "weakness" is obvious. The trouble is I never basically fooled myself. I knew it was time to retire *before* my drinking brought on a collapse that would shatter the "good old fellow" character. I was at a disadvantage in retirement. I could not take my people-pleasing very far into senior citizenry.

The sudden cessation of a need to please people affects all busy persons when they slip into retirement. Every breadwinner must be a people-pleaser to some extent whether he or she is forced to please a boss or a customer.

Once I had retired, I made motions toward pleasing only myself. This required reaching the goals I had set for myself many years earlier. I was ready and willing to sweat out all of the fine prose I had intended to write—

novels, plays, scripts, articles, short stories, nonfiction books.

In order to fulfill those dreams of being a creator, I would have to make the proper start each day before I sat down at a typewriter. I had not only read works by a batch of my favorite writers, but I studied their techniques and work patterns. I saw that each and every one of them had kindled that precious spark of genius by nipping from an uncorked bottle. All the writers whom I admired and respected and dreamed of emulating were living (or, alas, dead) proof that inspiration could be ignited by a liquid drug called alcohol.

I was hardly naive enough to imagine that creative ideas came through the act of kneeling and asking for it from a source as ethereal as liquor was real.

F. Scott Fitzgerald, who was captivating readers when he was barely out of college, once gave me guidance when he wrote, "When drunk, I make them pay and pay and pay and pay."

The list of great authors rumored to have preceded me into alcoholism was lengthy—Edgar Allan Poe, Robert Burns, Dylan Thomas, Evelyn Waugh, Sinclair Lewis, Eugene O'Neill, William Faulkner, Ernest Hemingway, John Steinbeck, John O'Hara, Ring Lardner, John Fowler, Jack London, Dashiell Hammett, Robert Benchley, Raymond Chandler. Who could ask for any more endorsements of the fact that brilliance comes in eighty-proof liquid fire?

I never bothered to inquire what alcohol had done to these men, as well as to their imaginations. The lengthy tomes that had been produced by them documented the conclusion that these writers took what they needed from hootch and beat down any of the attempts made by the stuff to create havoc. These artists, I truly believed, made slaves of alcohol, using it as Aladdin used the genie that came out of a vigorously rubbed bottle.

When I never could find the control handle for the "inspiration" that skidded rapidly into the boring state of being blotto, I reasoned that I had waited too long to be among the well-cultivated imbibers of literature. After all, many of them had found that magic, used it well, and died by their mid-forties.

I was not deterred. I simply became a morning drinker. I reasoned that nothing ever can be achieved without first making an attempt. I would never know the surge of literary fervor if I did not look for it at the earlist moment of any day. Unfortunately, I was like the inexperienced cook's first biscuits that squatted to rise and baked on the squat. I was finished physically and mentally before I could reach the thrill of ferreting out charming prose.

Naturally, all this brought self-rejection, feelings of inadequacy and deep self-pity. I became a sad alcoholic, a crying drunk. There was little pride in my sorrowful state. I savored many of my tear-jerking thoughts while hiding behind a newspaper which I pretended to read. Or listening, with face covered, to sad radio music in the pretense of getting into a writing mood. They were all my theme songs, for I related to them well. "Born to Lose," "I'll Never Smile Again," "I'm Dancing with Tears in My Eyes," "I Did It My Way."

I hit the well of loneliness, a bottomless supply of musical sobs and travail, when I came upon the all-country music station. All the anguish of unrequited love, deserted husbands, wives of unfaithful spouses and prison inmates were my brothers and sisters bound together by lyrics.

Once I heard the perfect song for meditating over things that never were but should have been when I was entranced by "Watching the Bubbles in My Beer." I smiled wryly at "What Made Milwaukee Famous Made a Loser Out of Me." And Yuletide jingle bells turned into dirges when I heard, "I'm Drinking My Christmas Dinner All Alone."

Since attaining sobriety, I have heard another song with which I would have related: "Here I Go Down That Wrong Road Again." It's the story of my misadventures. How many times I started a day determinedly vowing to travel the right road that whole day. But always, I got detoured. Taking that first drink each morning always sidetracked my good intentions.

Early in my recovery, I told others that there had been no insanity in my drinking. Eventually, it dawned on me that I had always prefaced each drink by a one-on-one talk with the bottle. Uncorking the jug, I would remind the container that its contents were being sought strictly for medicinal purposes. "Just for today, I need that eye-opener. Tomorrow, I'll surely not have the need. So, bottle, don't try to tempt me. Refrain from trying to inveigle me into yesterday's kind of ingestion. Or the day before's. Or the morning before that. This day it will be different. Just one, thank you."

The trouble was that I seemed unable to assure myself that the jug had heard. Uncertainty irked me. So, in order to answer my doubts, I would take down and uncork the bottle again.

Then, as long as the container was open, why waste all that effort just to ask a bottle if it had heard? Might as well pour another. And another. I never got to my typewriter cold sober.

There were times when my blood did not run high on alcohol content before noon. Frequently, the first drink came later. But it always came. Many a night I went to bed thinking, "Well, I *almost* made it."

Almost! The story of an alcoholic's life. We almost made it home by dinner time, almost failed to stop at the bar or liquor store, almost got that office promotion, almost paid the bills, almost remembered that anniversary date . . . almost . . . .

In one "almost" I rejoice. I almost did not quit drinking. It was so close a call that it is frightening today. I almost stayed in my old world until death came. I almost did not discover that there is life before death.

Remembering that helps me recall that "You have to grow, or you have to go."

Go where? I need no diagrams to spot that destination. If I fail to grow, I go back to the life from which I came.

Thank God, it was almost in self-defense that I was forced to delve deeply into the matter of character growth. I wanted to stay in my new world where, if I practiced certain principles, I just might always be able to say, "I'm the best me today that I've ever been."

4

Never Too Old to Change

I have had to face the question: "Was I unique as an alcoholic?" "Am I, today, nineteen years sober at this writing, different from other older alcoholics in the suffering and in the awakening to the reality of admitting and accepting?" Of course I am not.

All I know without reservation is that what I did and thought and usually lied about, I must share with others. The riches of the rewards resulting from living sober must be given away. Knowing that I am no rarity in the area of senior citizenry alcoholism, I must relate what happened and what solutions came from the act of humble and grateful seeking.

To those older problem drinkers and their concerned friends and loved ones, I accent the fact that humanity is a living assembly of people who are individuals. Each of us alcoholics, young or old, will drink and, hopefully, find recovery in his or her own way. And with multiple similarities. Addiction comes as the result of a misuse of the drug alcohol and sobriety is the achievement of each who chooses complete abstinence. How we oldsters come to the identical problem and our escape from it is not important nor are any attitudinal and behavioral differences vital. I did not do many of the things some other older alcoholics did, nor did they do everything I did.

I address with love all addicted readers and their bewildered and often-frustrated friends and relatives with a certainty that we must always look for identification and disregard differences. I am equally sure that older problem drinkers, once in recovery, are relieved to discover that all of us are not robots. If we all drank to excess and recovered in the exact same way, sobriety would bind us into an unhappy finale of boredom. And boredom is one of the reasons why we elderly topers sought a way out of tedium by guzzling.

Alcoholism is a disease that may come to a man or a woman of any age, societal status or beliefs. I, for one, have learned never to belabor or debate the disease theory. To puzzle over possible reasons why we fall victim to a disease which is mankind's third greatest killer (preceded in numbers only by cancer and heart disease) is a waste of time for us older alcoholics. We should avoid any disconcerting puzzlement that consumes hours, days, weeks, months and years which should be devoted to savoring the comfort, serenity, security, health and positive thinking which we diligently should try to find, through hospital units, treatment facilities and the fellowship of Alcoholics Anonymous. The best use I have found for admitting to having a disease called alcoholism is that it quickly and simply answers all questions such as "why," "how," "when" and "where" it developed and came close to destroying us. I have learned to end such ponderings by telling myself, "Why? All because I have a disease!" This preserves the use of time and lets me be concerned with living.

I've learned a lot about how others drank and sobered up while I was devoting much of my nineteen years of old-age sobriety to working with others in need of surrender. I have been schooled in living without alcohol by other elderly drinkers sharing happy abstinence. It was my good fortune to learn from and work with several therapists and counselors who specialized in the subject of geriatric addictive drinking. In A.A., members teach each other. I am grateful for having been a student of many teachers, whether they have been professional or recovery patients.

Among my "older-drinker" friends have been men and women in their mid-fifties and on up. One dear friend celebrated his eighty-fifth birthday in a recovery unit and emerged to lead a sober life. Another fellow A.A. who joined me in carrying the message to older alcoholics is a man named Sam. He has spent (to date) thirty-six years of sobriety from his fifty-eighth birthday.

I can assure retirees or near-retirees that if they begin sobriety with the need to care and share, they won't have to identify completely with all other ex-drinkers they meet. They won't have to agree on all voiced opinions but they will learn to disagree without being disagreeable. In A.A., we are told that we don't have to like everyone (even *anyone*) but we will *love* our program and all who follow it into a lasting sobriety.

Among fellow older alcoholics, there is the constant need for teachers. We understand when we are told "when the pupil is ready, the teacher will appear." And we come to agree that "when we find a teacher we find another friend." The book *Alcoholics Anonymous* promises that in the program "we will find new life-long friends."

That, dear friends, is what "fellowship" is all about. Love will be many things—being available, always understanding. All older alcoholics enjoy a program of mutuality where all who give will receive and the act of receiving always results in gracious giving.

Those who read about alcoholism or listen to talks on the subject are familiar with the information that the problems of each alcoholic affects the lives of an average of four other people who surround him or her as relatives or friends.

I realize that some of those who may be reading this book are nonalcoholics who are feeling deep frustration, dismay, anger and disgust with the older drinking person who "just won't listen."

Any one of us who recovers can tell you that you are not alone. The resistance that you get from a stubborn, denying older alcoholic is common with all who have lived to a ripe old age doing their own thing, one of which is drinking when, how and where they wish. If they don't want you to have an excuse to "heckle" them, they are experts at avoiding the issue or "turning you off" even when you are shouting and harassing.

You are not the first, not among a very few, who fail at getting your older friend or relative to admit and accept help. He or she is not rare in rebuffing you by saying, "Let me alone," "I'm okay," "I want to live my own life," or "If things really get bad, I can take care of the problem."

A troubled older alcoholic may even have given up, resigned himself to drinking to die. Yet many, many "hopeless" oldsters have been given a second life to live and a life that has a new purpose. If you despair, too, you will hasten the end for that person you love.

There often is a display of stigma among the people who surround elderly problem drinkers. If old boozers become aware of the feeling among others that they are unworthy of help, are a disgrace, may be a sinner, they will more likely retreat further into their loneliness and resignation to succumb to their disease. Of one thing a stigmatizer can be sure: if he or she speaks with disgust about an old toper and believes that the subject of discussion is so passed out that he or she will never hear the words, chances are great that the subject of such scorn will hear, will be affected by the words and never forgive.

Stigma is natural. Most of us have grown through a childhood and growing-up period when certain misfortunes to individuals brought on personal scorn and pity. Once, stigma was heaped on people with tuberculosis, epilepsy, "social diseases," physical handicaps, mental retardation and even stutterers and people who were "tongue-tied." These people felt their isolation by others who avoided contact. Our society has come a long way from that, but not all the way.

Stigma is most pronounced among nonalcoholics of the same ages as those who are obviously "drunks." Some researchers have found that this scorn is pronounced within large senior citizen villages. Elderly nonalcoholic people often are cruel in their attitude toward oldsters who "can't hold their liquor" or who behave "disgracefully."

For those unenlightened about alcoholism problems among older persons it is easy, often a matter of self-defense, to look down at an old drunk. Of course, they believe, "He became a drunk by choice," "She has no shame," "Why don't they straighten up?" Nonalcoholic seniors may even look upon an older tippler with a feeling of fear or embarrassment, thinking, "but for the grace of God, there go I."

How simple it is for stigma to devastate an older drinker. Most alcoholics of *all* ages develop an incredible low state of self-worth. Their esteem has been destroyed by enslavement from the drug they imbibe. They inevitably wind up feeling unworthy, rejected, untrusted, unneeded, unloved and doomed to failure. Usually, the feeling is unwarranted, but alcohol always has done strange things to the minds and bodies of older drinkers.

I can tell those stigmatizers who may regret their own display of disgust that many older alcoholics usually, upon seeing the display, accept it with little pain. We oldsters with booze in our veins have even come to the point of feeling stigma for ourselves if none is directed our way by neighbors or friends. Some bask in the glory of it. It makes some of us feel we are a sort of success, are certainly different, and nourish some degree of masochism.

That the specter of stigma can lead to strange situations in the field of senior alcoholism was made clear to me and to another older recovering alcoholic who was serving on the public information committee of a local chapter of the National Council on Alcoholism.

We had spoken so often at meetings about the hidden segment status of older alcoholics that an influential member of the committee set up a small luncheon for us with a few officials whose duties included serving senior citizen centers.

We asked if one agency served the city's senior centers with newsletters and information sheets. Assured that the nice lady at the meeting did just that, we asked if she would include in the next directive the fact that there were two older recovering drinkers who were willing to visit any center that would like to hear about the big problem of the elderly drinking too much.

The answer was no.

We asked, "No what?"

"We can't send such information."

"Why?" was a natural query.

The answer was understandable. "Those who frequent such centers are depressed enough by feeling the onus of growing old. We don't wish to add to their feeling of being unimportant by adding the possibility that they might also be alcoholics."

We couldn't argue against that, even if it was hard to accept.

Many a would-be helper learns early from sad experience that older drinkers can seldom be shamed, threatened, flattered or seduced by promises into accepting help. Shouting does no good; it usually accents the stubborn resentment of the drinker. A roomful of tears has little effect. Actually, weeping will usually convince the smug old deniers that they have shown a "do-gooder" that they can't be ordered around or "treated like a child." It can become a matter of pride for oldsters. They are sure that they have won a minor battle. They may be harder to deal with in the future. No matter how tightly alcoholism's grip on them becomes, elderly topers continue to build up the grandiosity that makes a "surrender" harder and harder to accomplish.

It might seem effective and obvious to one who is unknowledgeable about the character of an older alcoholic that a quick deterrent to drinking would be to hide the bottles or pour their contents down a drain. The drinker will only be inconvenienced. He or she *will* replenish the supply. There are enabling friends, fellow drinkers or fast delivery from a liquor store. And the older drinker will probably never forget, or again trust, the bottle thief. The confiscator will have lost another round in "saving" the drinker. By nature, the alcoholic is suspicious of do-gooders whom he or she considers a threat to "happiness."

One of the great tragedies in the efforts to get help for older drinkers is the practice of those close to the drinker to be "enablers," believing they must keep up the drinker's supply and protect the drinker's secret or the drinker will die. They refrain from asking advice from experts on alcoholism because they are ashamed of their "family drunk." Embarrassment is a mistaken concern. Chances are great that everyone who comes into even casual contact with the senior citizen who drinks knows the truth. Enabling usually prevents the outsider who could lift a voice from speaking up. The more a relative enables, the more a person who might help gets the impression that the family wants the alcoholic to drink himself or herself to death or be hospitalized.

Older drinkers who look back from a rich sobriety to the horror and pain of their drinking are likely to regret the alibi-making their families did with friends, neighbors or casual acquaintances such as the mailman or the plumber. Many oldsters knew at the time what was going on and were aware of being protected. That knowledge bolstered feelings of being an artful and successful deceiver who was master of his or her fate. Obviously, enabling provides many subtle deterrents to a life of abstinence for an elderly drinker.

It is apparent that covering up cannot encourage the honesty required for making it in a program like

Alcoholics Anonymous. When family members enable or concoct alibis for an older alcoholic, they are really telling the alcoholic that they believe he or she *has* to drink.

The cunning of alcoholics is next to incredible. How their egos swell when they see they are fooling, even betraying, the alibiers. They have no respect for "moralists," even among family members. And they know that they can escape criticism, pity and concern from others by simply retorting to suggestions that they get help by saying, "This is a free country. Get off my back."

The older drinker's suspicion of would-be helpers is magnified when the one who approaches him or her is a recovering alcoholic, even if the A.A. Twelfth-Stepper is of the drinker's age. (The Twelfth Step says, "Having had a spiritual awakening as the result of these Steps, we tried to carry this message to alcoholics.") This is why when a family member calls an A.A. central office to request a visit from a member to old Uncle Joe, he or she is so often told, "It won't work unless Uncle Joe himself calls us for help."

Tough, denying oldsters with alcohol in their bellies will have no regard for one who has been a "quitter" and given up the friendly bottle. They seldom believe A.A. long-timers. How many times have we heard, in A.A., a newcomer older alcoholic says to the twenty-year sober member, "I don't believe it," only to feel a spark of recognition and friendliness toward a member who announces, "I came in two days ago."

Everyone who has recovered from an addiction, especially those who work with problem drinkers at treatment facilities, know that surrender, acceptance and just wanting sobriety is vital for any beginning. The personal desire has to be greater than the personal pain.

For centuries everyone who has wanted to give lifesaving help to another person has known the old adage, "You can lead a horse to water but you can't make him drink."

In A.A. and hospital units, the last word has been changed to "thirsty." The older drinker must be thirsty for life before death.

The best thing someone concerned about the drinking of Aunt Abby can do as a starter is to learn something about alcoholism and the personality of its victims. Not much knowledge is necessary. It is readily available. A.A., the Alcoholism Council or the nearest treatment facility or hospital for alcoholism will quickly supply verbal advice or a pamphlet. Once the concerned person knows how easily he or she can say the wrong words through ignorance, the nearer is the day recovery begins for a friend.

The older alcoholic must be impelled or encouraged to ask for help. No matter how isolated, stubborn, resistant and hazy the drinker may be, there is always (not just almost always) some person to whom he or she will listen. The family member or friend must find that individual. The trusted one could be a minister, a doctor, a former favorite teacher, member of the clergy, old classmate, fraternity brother or sorority sister, childhood pal, an idol from the sports or entertainment field. Surprisingly often, this trusted friend, with knowledge of what to ask and suggest, can induce the most stubborn, most denying and befuddled drinker to "see the light." Always with love . . . always.

There is a method of getting through to the oldest drug-addicted man or woman to effect a self-centered request to get sober. Its successes have been many and amazing. It has been written about in periodicals and books. And it is soul-stirring. It is intervention. In an intervention, the alcoholic's concerned friends and family members with the guidance of a trained therapist, one by one lovingly confront the alcoholic with the evidence that he or she needs help. A.A., the Alcoholism Council and/or a local treatment facility can provide information on intervention.

Intervention usually leads to admission to an alcoholism unit of a hospital. Here, bottle-scarred oldsters will find companionship and love. They will learn that there is no generation gap in recovery. They will mix with men and women their own age and all of them will join with patients of *all* ages. They will learn from those they once considered "brainless brats" and some whom they even considered "senile old nuts." They will learn the joy of again being a pupil who needs teachers. It will be the beginning of a perpetual classroom from which they never want to be graduated.

Above all, they will learn that they never need to be bored, lonely or feel unneeded again. They will "make lifelong friends," as A.A.'s "Big Book" states. They will find that they have not only saved their own lives but have made their once-miserable lives worth saving.

Hospital units usually encourage after-care. Such follow-ups will be constant "rap" sessions. Older drinkers, now free of bondage and with freedom of choice, will find involvement the cure for boredom. Caring and sharing will become the answer to loneliness. The love which always comes to people who need people—and who find the right people—will be a deterrent to all thoughts of no longer being needed by fellow human beings. Those three newly found assets will be with them as they get back into society and discover that a miracle has permitted them to again join the human race and achieve one of the most rewarding joys of living with others—to always, always be kind.

• ■ ■

5

What Kind of Folk Are We?

Early in my years of recovery from senior citizen alcoholism, I was reminded of my many years of constant denial and I learned that this was no practice on which older drinkers held a monopoly. Alcoholics, young and old alike, can be described as people who invariably never admit to having had more than a couple of drinks. So easily does denial begin.

Most experts agree that the number one symptom of alcoholism is this denial. Some laugh-seekers assert that alcoholism is the only disease that continually tells the drinker he doesn't have it.

If the older drinker is constantly relying on excuses for his or her drinking, on alibis, cop-outs and cover-ups then it's time to admit that there may be a problem. But how hard we older drinkers work at a refusal to admit and accept the reality that we are powerless over such an insignificant thing as a drink of alcoholic beverage.

Such acceptance would seem natural. After all, by the time we elderly drinkers have reached retirement age, we have gone through a lot of living battles and won most of them. We have coped with costly rejection, hard-to-take losses of valued assets and prestige. We have been betrayed by friends many times and have survived. However, we cannot even consider the fact that a liquid that has comforted us so often and potently can be a false friend. We have faith in an unrecognizable enemy which we consider a friend.

One of our attitudes about our drinking is the refusal to admit that drinking alcohol has been the source of the shame, guilt, remorse and regret we experience after a binge that has hurt and saddened those we love or someone who is important to our well-being. We can blame those around us, even ourselves. But we cannot easily accept the possibility that alcohol is not the magic potion it always appeared to be once we took another first drink.

Was I a freak as an older drinker who had lost the ability to control my intake? Was I different? If ever I felt unable to identify with the multitudes of retirement-years drinkers in a particular pattern of imbibing, I awakened to the fallacy of thinking I was different when I began seeking help. I wasn't. Statistics are important now only in telling me that I never was alone as a "typical old drunk" and that I can possibly carry to countless other oldsters the message that there *is* a way out.

But, for what it can mean to the reader, experts on old-age alcoholism estimate that 10 percent of all of the thirty-two million men and women over sixty and the twenty-five million aged over sixty-five (population estimates from the National Council on Aging) are alcoholic. That covers those who do not drink (one third of all citizens are nondrinkers) as well as nonalcoholic social drinkers. It is accepted that the incidence of alcoholism for all elderly drinkers is 15 percent. This indicates that I am among some three million Americans over sixty who are alcoholic. In the Medicare bracket of over-sixty-five, there are two and a half million who are addicted to a drug that most of us never knew was a drug and which we imbibed with what we called "our freedom of choice."

Researchers tell us something that really wouldn't have alarmed me to know when I was drinking. That is that only about 2 percent of those older drinkers are living soberly today. That fact alone tells me that I never was an "exception" but always was a part of a big, big problem.

Today, the realization that I managed to climb out of a pit I was sharing with a few million fellow men and women impels me to try never to ask, mournfully, "Why did I become an alcoholic?" but to ask exhultantly "Why am *I* sober? Why among all those older alcoholics have I been freed of the compulsion to drink for more than nineteen senior-citizen years?" That, I tell myself repeatedly, is what gratitude really means.

If the subject needs amplification, we can be sure the numbers of elderly alcoholics are going to increase in the coming years. Today men and women are living longer. The ranks of persons over sixty will swell and more will attain the century mark in longevity. If 10 percent of the growing number continues to become alcoholic, the numbers game will not decrease. If awareness of the seriousness of alcoholism among older Americans continues to increase as it has done during the past two decades, hopefully the 2 percent recovery expectancy will grow. Today, there are more doctors who are knowledgeable about old-age alcoholism. More elderly addicts are finding their way into more and more treatment centers and membership in Alcoholics Anonymous for the old and middle-aged and the very young is increasing month by month.

The older drinker *can* be reached. Maybe knowing a little more about him or her—and me—can help.

What are we older drinkers like?

To begin with, no man or woman who ever became a hidden alcoholic did all of the exact things every other senior citizen guzzler did or will do. Our exact way of thinking, our attitudes, our behavior, our tastes, even our recoveries, have never been identical. Perhaps not even similar, excepting that each one has to surrender, to admit, to accept, to turn problems to a Higher Power, to accept help from fellow A.A. members and from that Higher Power and to practice the steps of A.A. to the best of his or her ability in his or her own way. Had all done precisely the same things in the same way A.A. would be a fellowship for robots who perform with no deviation. Alcoholics surely are people who enjoy being and behaving as individuals.

If A.A. and other recovery programs are free from boredom, that in itself is a change for the better among oldsters. Survey all older alcoholics and the fact will loom large that, to some degree, every older alcoholic seeks the presumed uplifting provided by alcohol through suffering the pains of boredom coupled with the feeling of rejection by a society that once found him or her useful.

Loneliness did not require a typical older alcoholic like me to be in solitude or live alone. It has been said that a naturally lonely older drinker would be lonely sitting in a stadium with ninety thousand other spectators watching a football game. I identify with that.

Most of us senior drinkers were, and often still are depressed and stressed because we feel we are no longer considered useful. That feeling is more devastating than feeling unloved. In a world which we believe has passed us by and has surrendered to younger men and women whom we believe only give an impression of being more alert, more capable and more imaginative, we naturally are sure that society is unfair to us. We feel we still have much to offer and we become restless in the fact of retirement restrictions. In such a state of mind, we naturally turn our attention to the greatest restorer of self-worth we believe exists—alcohol.

One of the most certain results of feeling lonely, bored and unneeded is the rapid decrease of self-esteem. I started life feeling less than everyone around me. I believed I really deserved to have been born on the wrong side of the tracks socially. I grew up sure that I was unworthy, unqualified and unable to achieve great things. Like others, I fought that feeling all my life and became more and more of a selfish people-pleaser, sure that if I connived to make people like me and want to help me the more they would see that I got things I didn't think I could earn.

If we older alcoholics drank to give an artificial inflation to a low self-esteem, our belief in the emotional benefits of using liquor to gain confidence, and our dependence on a drug which we couldn't ignore, afforded most of us an assurance that we were crafty enough to keep others from suspecting a possible problem. Besides, we were always sure we could stop when our drinking became anywhere close to serious. Our defense was the steps we took to keep our behavior hidden.

Hiding the truth was not hard to accomplish. Without knowing that our efforts would actually make us a hidden segment of a national problem, we often leaned toward caution in being seen to overuse liquor.

The result was that we older drinkers seldom made statistical charts.

While numerous recovering senior-citizen alcoholics have spent many occasions in traffic court or jail for drunk driving, a far greater number drank all through retirement years and into A.A. without receiving a citation. Because my own severest drinking took place during the two years from retirement at sixty-eight and entrance into A.A. at seventy, I never faced a judge. But, of course, I could have.

Countless others also escaped the indignity of being a drunken old motorist. During my sober years in A.A., I often sensed the possibility that had I been sentenced to A.A. earlier or even been embarrassed into taking that step to find sobriety, I might not have drunk until I was seventy.

In recovery, we do not dwell on "What if" and "If only." But to all of us who make it to sobriety comes a chance to understand some reasons why we were hidden for so long. Older drinkers do not *have* to drive to a liquor store or bar. The smartest of us realize that, so long as we have the cash, liquor stores will deliver.

The average older drinker cannot really afford bar prices so he or she doesn't leave home to get drunk. Even those in mansions and penthouses, with servants to attend to their drunkenness, usually prefer passing out in the comfort of their own beds.

Solitary drinking is the best choice for a majority of elderly tipsters. The wiser of us always fear falling down; too many of our friends have suffered broken bones and often died as a result. Drunk as we occasionally were, we were influenced by the innate desire for self-preservation.

Loneliness is the major choice of the older drunkard. I have met more than one recovered alcoholic in their later years who have confessed that during some of their best drinking days they refused to answer the telephone or doorbell.

Few elderly men or women ever get arrested for "common drunkenness." What about those old sots and unkempt hags that dress the backgrounds of skid row scenes in the movies and on TV?

They really exist, of course. But researchers have stated for decades that less than 3 percent of *all* drunks are to be found in all the skid rows of this nation. So much for stereotypes.

For decades, it has been possible to hide the major affliction of men and women who are hospitalized for alcoholism. Kind doctors, mindful of the fact that truth might embarrass nice family members needlessly, have always had the privilege of booking a drunken grandma into a hospital room for ailments other than those resulting from overindulgence of the bottle. And rightfully so. It is a fact that 81 percent of every senior citizen alcoholic has a serious ailment *other* than alcoholism.

If hospitalization of older alcoholics ever could have been termed subterfuge, it no longer is necessary. A vast number of hospitals have alcoholism units into which many an old-timer heavy into the ingestion of liquor is freely admitted to the relief and gratitude of family members. Treatment costs can be picked up by Medicare and private insurance policies.

Now old Aunt Sarah and Uncle Joe are counted along with teen-agers and middle-agers with no separate classifications. Secrecy today is out of date.

But awareness of alcohol problems among the elderly still is sadly low, even if there has been some progress.

For people like me who never believed it could happen to them, there was no reason to go looking for books or magazine and newspaper essays on the threat to older drinkers of a potent problem with a potion that was socially acceptable.

TV spots flashed on late at night for the benefit of the Alcoholism Council and Alcoholics Anonymous (free public service plugs). Some early paid announcements about alcohol treatment by hospital units did not reach me because they concerned younger victims, which I believed excluded me. Booze could be a serious problem for someone else, not me.

Because drinking by elderly alcoholics was so hidden, stories in newspapers and magazines about problem drinkers always gave attention to the younger generation, women and drunk drivers. I don't remember ever reading a story or seeing a special on TV about the drinking retirees. Nineteen years later, I still can't recall such pieces.

It was natural for me, if anyone ever alluded to alcoholism among the elderly, to say or merely tell myself, "There can't be much of a problem about guys like me or I'd be reading about it in the newspapers or seeing alarming TV news reports."

What I did see were those thirst-impelling commercials about beer. Did I ever salivate, since beer was the only palatable alcoholic drink for me. I drank "hard liquor" only for the intoxication it brought.

Later, well into A.A., that appeal of beer commercials resulted in a laughing experience for me. I related it only to keep reminding myself that we in A.A. never came to recovery to get somber, but sober. Laughing is one of the great attractions of A.A. for me. As I have laughed, I have often reminded myself that people who laugh live longer and a day without laughter is not worthy of being lived.

What I told an A.A. long-timer one day during my first year was, "Beer commercials upset me. What am I supposed to do when I see one of those flashy commercials and think of nice, cold beer going down?" He just grunted, "Keep on looking and think of warm beer coming up."

I laughed. I identified. How often warm beer did erupt.

I was not alone in drinking heavily in ignorance of what risks I was taking with my aging body. It is obvious that there are many oldsters drinking today in a state of unenlightenment about reality as I once was.

I cannot criticize those who don't see in a fellow drinker who is stoned, silly and disgusting a "bad example" to whom they can compare themselves. Maybe I always feared that risk of possibly seeing in a drunken and suffering crony something of myself. Seeing the differences and not the similarities is a shortcoming shared by all alcoholics, male and female.

Of course, it is needless to look back in sobriety to the neglected chances to talk as a fellow older alcoholic to one who was as deep into his problem as was I. But we can't look back with regrets, and certainly not with despair. Today, I can only atone by making efforts to nudge the awareness of the problem for one or more who have a chance to do something about their addiction—with the satisfaction of having made that step through their own choice and with an acceptance of help from another old alcoholic.

As the problem of alcohol's effect on the process of aging becomes clearer, some knowledgeable people do write and speak about the simple facts of aging. Reading and listening will be a starter for an older alcoholic.

The road to sobriety for one who is slowly drinking him- or herself to a premature death can begin with the general knowledge that aging means a constant decrease in the viability for living and constant increase in vulnerability to those enemies of better living and comfortable aging. Then, we may suddenly see that alcohol is one of those enemies that take advantage of any vulnerability.

As time passes year by year, there is a constant potential for a general slowing down of all functions of our bodies. That tendency is the target for a takeover by the drug alcohol and its ability to addict the user.

Aging, we read, is not in itself a necessarily disabling situation. We can make it a liability only by injecting that process of growing older with a chemical that breeds excessiveness and obsession. Nature intends mankind to develop and utilize a healthy balance in aging properly. Ingestion of alcohol always tips that balance toward the negative.

I had really not become, until my retirement at sixty-eight, a daily drinker who started each morning with an eye-opener and got drunker, then more sober a few times until the nightly passing out and the awakening in the hours just after midnight with the shakes, the sweats and the fearfulness that sent me to a big leather chair to indulge in the prayer, "God help me."

That happened in the space of only two years' time. It was contrary to the few things I had read about alcoholism, one of which was the estimate by experts that it took from five to fifteen years for a drinker to progress through the stages of powerlessness over alcohol to the end result of chronic alcoholism.

My conclusion was that, even if I continued to progress toward what could never happen to me, I had at least three more years of drinking. During that time, I could wise up and simply stop drinking.

Somewhere during those hazy two years, I failed to see or hear a learned observation that the older drinkers and the very young imbibers have one thing in common—at both extremes in age, the user could readily emerge a real alcoholic in from eighteen months to three years. When I heard that, after years of happy sobriety, I was surprised to read that this addictableness shared by the old and the young indicated that drinkers in the two age extremes shared a common search—the young to find themselves, the elderly to regain lost identities.

No wonder I had identified at seventy with the fourteen-year-old leader of the first A.A. meeting I attended.

I liked that sharing of an identity search better than another observation: that the young drink for psychological reasons, the older for physical benefit.

I'm glad I got to know some facts about myself before it was too late. And what I didn't know *was* hurting me while I drank.

6

Had We But Known

As a mystery story buff ever since my boyhood discovery of Edgar Allen Poe and Arthur Conan Doyle, I have enjoyed all the detective novel forms. This includes the school of writing, mastered by Mary Roberts Reinhart, known as "Had I But Known." Somewhere early in such a novel, the first-person narrator always intrigues the reader by sighing in print words to the effect, "If only I had known then what was to happen and who was to victimize me. . . ."

Most older alcoholics, like the threatened heroine of a novel, never suspected how far down the scale of addiction they were going or how alcohol was altering their good lives. A degree of ignorance about the reality of alcoholism often surrounds the elderly problem drinker. Out of the unawareness on the part of large areas of society came misconceptions about senior citizens' drinking.

I often conjecture about the possibilities of relief that might have ensued from stressing truths (even thrusting facts down the throats of older drinkers) to drinkers and their families and associates. But in recovery, drinkers seldom find comfort in asking "What if?" The A.A. slogan "One day at a time" tells us that we may occasionally "visit" our past to remind us of what it was like and needs no longer be, but it is dangerous to try to relive the past.

"If only" voices had been lifted higher with cautions and "if only" we had all listened more and denied less, the accepted conclusion that an "old drunk is doomed to certain death" might have enjoyed less popularity. Much of the blame lies with us older drinkers who refused to listen even when voices rose loud and clear.

Today, older alcoholics can be convinced that their constant denial of alcoholism is always just a defense against admitting and accepting. The sly and crafty use of excuses usually is prompted by an aversion to admitting the disease of alcoholism. To accept the word *alcoholic* was to brand oneself as a failure, a quitter, an undesirable, one to be pitied and an immoral weakling. If we who live in that state of mind had ever, in our cups, heard the words, "you don't have to say you're an alcoholic, just that you have a *desire* to quit drinking" many of us might have found *no escape* in believing *we* were different because we were among the elderly.

Not until we get to A.A. do we discover that few of us had any connection to skid row bums. We learned that we were something known as "high bottom alcoholics" who had not lost our dignity and hocked our watches. No matter how long the realization is in coming to us, we can freely accept the fact that we oldsters were not solely to blame for the hiddenness within which we drank toward death.

Misconceptions about older drinkers are bountiful and begin with a general repulsion to accepting the incredible impression of kindly, old cookie-baking grandma or that gift-bearing, story-telling and lovable old grandpa could ever be tagged a drunk. Who can suspect that the "dignity of the elderly" is on shaky ground? There is a popular worldwide image of grand-mothers and grandfathers and it isn't that of an alcoholic.

There also are, it is sad to admit, those younger relatives and blame-dodging friends of elderly drinkers who are far too busy maintaining their careers or social involvements to accept responsibility for pursuing the "lost cause" of trying to get hopeless drunks back on their feet.

It is simple to find loved ones who just can't be bothered about a soul-saving act that belongs to the clergy and civic organizations. It is not unusual to hear some who should be concerned remark, "Hell, he's far less trouble when he's drunk." Sure he is. Sure!

It is easy not to see evidence that nice, gentle and often affluent oldsters have drinking problems. One researcher was told by managers of a vast senior citizen community that there was hardly any out-of-control drinking in the area. But rubbish collectors judged that a third of all they picked up weekly consisted of empty liquor bottles and beer cans. Hidden indeed!

Most misconceptions, however, are existent not because society doesn't care to know. They just seem obvious and free from disguise.

Probably the most errant conceptions about older drinkers are that they can taper off from heavy drinking to abstinence without much difficulty and that there surely can't be many older alcoholics, because the disease is so serious that it kills long-time drinkers long before they reach old age.

It is not necessary to list all of the easy excuses of those surrounding the older drinker as to why he or she has good reasons to overindulge. But, some of them go like this:

It's too late to help him. He's far too old to get sober.

It would be cruel to deprive the poor woman of one of the last pleasures remaining in her life.

Old alcoholics are hurting nobody but themselves.

They've earned the right to drink the way they wish.

At his age, a little drink can't hurt him.

She's got good reasons to drink.

I'm sure that liquor helps relieve his pains.

All her family drank; she's inherited the problem.

His friends all drink. He's in good company.

She's escaping boredom. There's little left for her to do.

He's just stubborn. He could quit if he really wanted to.

Older drinkers are aware of these excuses and take advantage of them. When friends or relatives wash their hands of the problem so easily, the drinker is sure that nobody cares. At the same time, those who try to press help upon the elderly alcoholic, in the eyes of the drinker, are insincere "do-gooders."

Many senior alcoholics wind up in a treatment center without suspecting the severity of their addiction. Thousands are more surprised at the doctor's diagnoses than their families are. Yet, perhaps, numbering more than the unsuspecting are those who submit to hospitalization because they have become aware of their addiction. They have tried to quit, perhaps only *dreamed* of quitting. The lucky ones know that, when alcoholism has beaten them to their knees, the best thing to do is remain on their knees and begin praying for help. Today more older compulsive users of alcohol have discarded their sensitiveness to stigma, stopped denying and agreed to try for sobriety. One of the miracles of today's caring about elderly alcoholics is the honesty that enters the consciousness of old drinkers and of those surrounding them.

Proof that awareness within the older alcoholic has developed in recent years is found in the results of a survey made of elderly recovering alcoholics by a blue ribbon commission on alcoholism to learn the reasons why the drinkers themselves believe they resisted treatment for so long. The following deterrents to seeking help appeared in 95 percent of the responses:

— Denial of a problem with alcohol

— Society's free acceptance of drinking

— Awareness of the alcoholic stigma

— Overmedication with other soporific drugs while drinking

— Health problems which the drinker believed could be made endurable by ingestion of alcohol

— The cover-ups of their drinking by family members

— Feelings of loneliness and boredom

— An apparent lack of community interest in them

These replies point to the fact that denial *is* more often a defense of secret problems than is suspected by loved ones. When a heavy drinker refrains from crying out for help, it often is the result of the oldster feeling that maybe he or she isn't in trouble since nobody else seems to notice. Sadly, the alcoholic may be waiting for someone to validate his or her own creeping suspicion of a possible problem. And there are so many simple signs that can alert any family member or friend to the fact that Mom, Dad, Uncle, Aunt, Granddad or Grandma is having a problem with booze that it is surprising that more confrontations are withheld.

It is hard to believe that the older drinker is so expert at deceit that he or she can keep unnoticed such obvious signs of drunkenness as a breath laden with the odor of liquor, a loss of appetite, constant sleeplessness, a growing loss of memory, the evidence of burns or bruises or fractures caused by falls and bumping into things, a flushed face, growing depression and hostility, neglect of appearance and cleanliness and constant errors in simple paperwork.

Such important *minor* things can be more revealing than completely passing out, which usually happens when the drinker is not in contact with neighbors or relatives.

Many a friend or relative of an older alcoholic has used such minor behavior and attitudes to come to a decision about a drinking friend. There are such keen observers of possible problems as those who see signs of a growing problem even in studied overneatness, another clever cover-up of alcoholics.

Frustrated loved ones often protest that the elderly alcoholic is so stubborn and adamant about not "confessing" that he or she would rather die than admit to being an alcoholic. But in spite of all the denial, there are still limits to the utilization of lies, deceit and deception. Many caring people have been surprised at how easy success has been when they act positively and find the drinker ready and willing to surrender. The importance of willingness cannot be minimized. It usually is the key word to admitting and accepting.

Those who love older alcoholics can be relieved and encouraged to continue all-out efforts by acting with the knowledge that few, if any, alcoholics are ever really contented and happy at feeling miserable, unworthy, guilty, in pain or undeserving of outside efforts to help them. Extreme self-pity usually is a false front that the drinker inwardly wishes to lose. It may be an astounding discovery for the caring outsider when he or she learns that the "hopeless" alcoholic secretly is looking for a chance to laugh at the image of an unpleasant old piece of humanity he or she tries so hard to be when drunk.

No matter how far down the scale their attitude and physical condition may descend, alcoholics like anyone else, are reluctant to consider themselves immoral or beyond hope. And through any alcoholic haze, they are ever aware of love when it is honest and outpouring.

Those friends of the elderly drinker who may be uncertain about the extent of seriousness of the senior's use of alcohol can find a guide for assurance by reading a copy of "Twenty Questions" about alcoholism that is available at most A.A. meetings or offices of the National Council on Alcoholism and in hospitals where alcoholism is treated. If the drinker answers yes to any three of the questions, he or she is told that he or she is addicted and should enter a program aimed at sobriety.

These twenty questions have been adapted for a self-test by older heavy drinkers. A number of elderly recovered alcoholics have had a hand in creating such a list, which goes as follows:

1. Do you dislike or condemn yourself after you have drunk to intoxication?

2. Do you drink with an attitude about life of "It doesn't really matter" or "What's the use?"

3. Do you frequently miss such prescheduled activities as social events, doctor's appointments or dates with hairdressers or barbers?

4. Do you often use the money needed to pay the rent or bills to buy alcohol?

5. Are there occasions when drinking is more important than your relations with your family, friends or neighbors?

6. Have you ever suffered injury from falls, burns or cuts when you were drinking?

7. Is drinking the answer for coping with boredom when you have time on your hands and little to do?

8. Have you ever experienced a blackout as a result of drinking, causing you to have a complete loss of memory for days, even weeks at a time?

9. Has your doctor ever expressed concern about your use of alcohol?

10. When your self-confidence is low, do you turn to alcohol to rebuild your self-worth?

11. Do you wake up during the night and get up to pour yourself a drink?

12. Do you have to consume a drink to get to sleep?

13. Does alcohol enable you to participate in special events and holidays?

14. Are your relationships with neighbors, family or friends deteriorating because of your drinking?

15. After you drink do you find it advisable to avoid contact with friends who are not drinking buddies?

16. Does consumption of alcohol result in your inability to make personal decisions promptly?

17. Do you prefer to drink alone and do you deny to others that you drink excessively?

18. Is alcohol your answer to covering up fears, worry or sadness?

19. Have you ever refused to answer the telephone or doorbell because you do not want contact when you are intoxicated?

20. Have you ever been hospitalized for medical problems which have resulted from your drinking?

If answering such questions threatens a drinker's assurance that he or she is not an alcoholic, it's time for some self-examination about the reasons he or she does drink. Many alcoholics in denial maintain that alcohol is the solution—and that other people, places and things are the problem. The honest self-assessment these questions ask for can be the first step toward the realization that alcohol itself intensifies the feelings of loneliness, emptiness and unproductivity we seniors experience, and that alcohol isolates us from the people, places and things that can make life at any age rich and rewarding.

7

We Prime Targets

I was a sad old drunk. I cried often. I had lots of company in those years. Both male and female. Today, despite all the progress in reaching older alcoholics with messages of hope and help, there still are many who drink amid sadness. They need not cry although their need for tears is understandable.

The old alcoholic has good reasons for despair while his disease is progressing from social drinking into acute stages. Reasons that are both emotional and physical. (As the old song says, we can't have one without the other.)

Sadness keeps most of us drinking to live, then to die. The more we wept, the more we drank. And the greater the intake, the more overflowing the tears.

There should have been a revelation about both the need for tears and the cause for them in my case because my favorite song was "Born to Lose." Supplementing that song were "The Bottle Let Me Down," and "I'm So Lonesome I Could Cry."

Not all older alcoholics cry a majority of the time, either before or after they cross that well-known invisible line. None of us can cry all of the time any more than we can stay drunk all of the time.

In time, crying became a part of old-age alcoholism as much as being the "life of the party" may have once been our pleasure in the early social drinking era. We always saw reasons for being sad because of the rejections we suffered, the betrayals we felt had come from society and the lies we were sure had been showered upon us by those who promised us happiness and joy in retirement.

Why shouldn't we have felt lied to when, on numerous occasions, we moaned aloud to ourselves with words meant for unhearing ears, "It's not what you folks said old age would be like." The "you folks" were writers, lecturers, TV commentators, counselors, pastors and, above all, those who conceived those comforting and appealing advertisements that flooded all areas of the media.

We soon-to-be problem drinkers approached retirement or entered into it ready and anxious to believe promises and follow advice. But the encouraging words we read and heard never contained the caution, "All these goodies can't come true IF you don't attend to your inner self and find ways to fill up your life and IF you drink to avoid your problems."

When all the delightful promises did not come into our lives, we were eager to blame the "lying experts" and never the liquid we consumed or ourselves for the compulsiveness and excessiveness we practiced.

When we first heard the truths, "You will live longer when you are happily married, sleep well and exercise," how much we agreed and how grateful we were for the assurances.

Either we didn't listen well or nobody bothered to tell us plainly that a happy marriage was hardly possible when our drinking caused destruction, separation, discord and possible divorce. Sleeping well was impossible when drinking caused us to awaken late at night with a pounding heart, the shakes and the sweats because we had passed out long before regular bedtime. And how seldom did we have time to engage in healthful exercise when so many hours were devoted to a passed-out condition which left us sprawled immobily on a chair, on a sofa, or stretched out on the tiles of the bathroom.

Naturally we saw blame only for those who held out false promises to "gullible old drinkers." No blame ever was thrown at what we consumed so blatantly or at ourselves for putting our trust in a false friend.

With a feeling of justification, we cried out, when a scapegoat was needed, "Why didn't someone ever tell us that 'You'll live longer only if you DON'T become a slave to alcohol'?" But such words never were applicable until after we had admitted to our alcoholism.

Few of us weepers ever shed tears over the truth that, as older drinkers, we were prime targets for a disease called alcoholism. While researchers tell us that two-thirds of all older alcoholics are life-long drinkers who have survived into senior citizenry, evidence does exist that a great many men and women begin to use alcohol to excess in their fifties, when liquor is needed to assist in the solving of problems both physical and emotional.

In either case, the turning point in the drinking life of the majority still is when retirement becomes an actuality. It is then when aging and alcoholism compound each other the most, when we are sitting ducks for a problem we insist on denying.

The stress of retirement can begin years before we are, willingly or resistingly, "put out to pasture." Some of us are well prepared for retirement. Too many are not. Only a few of us come from industry, professions and businesses where there are preretirement courses to advise busy oldsters about what problems they will face in their leisure years and how to cope with them. But woefully little of such preparation is directed at warning about the rapid approach of a drinking problem.

A great many retirees aren't prepared for leisure years that can bring boredom, loneliness and a keen sense of having been relegated to uselessness by the busy world that seems to have passed them by. Among us are countless men and women who have few real hobbies. Playing checkers, bowling on the green, collecting, bridge or gin games, even golf, if used as a *substitute* for really connecting with other people and achieving something personally meaningful, can become tedious and uninteresting. And whatever hobby a busy practitioner of gracious social drinking has, it can easily become a losing competitor with the bottle.

Many an older man or woman has sought comfort in alcohol when grief became a big factor in living after the loss of a mate. Soon, this person is a candidate for rapid dependency on alcohol for making life worth living.

Psychologists have stated that the first two years after an older citizen has lost a wife or husband are critical in terms of what will substitute for the departed partner. Men are considered to be two and a half times more likely to deterioriate emotionally and physically than a woman after a spouse's death. The frequency of substituting alcohol for a lost love relationship should not be surprising. What is more readiliy available and socially accepted?

The senior citizen who begins to drink more often and more heavily recedes quickly into a loneliness from which he or she can emerge only by the realization that people need people. If the attempt to escape boredom and being unneeded motivates senior citizens to enter the world of volunteerism, that activity must be one in which they relate with the other volunteers. For one who is not an alcoholic, that sense of belonging can be almost anything. For alcoholics it can only be a recovery program. Until they come to that realization, senior drinkers will suffer the emotional and physical pains of their disease. They will suffer these pains until they surrender to a disease that comes from a bottle, a disease that is rated as one of the eight most prevalent health problems for the elderly, the older drinker and people around him. They will suffer until they become aware of the folly of denial and the need for acceptance and humility.

Older drinkers need to not only get their emotional defects straightened out but to also make sure that their attitudes concerning their physical being are on a reality course.

All humans begin to build a physical intolerance to alcohol at birth. Tolerance to drugs steadily decreases the longer a person lives—even when the person is not drinking. In addition, the intake of alcohol increases an unhealthy appetite for *all* drugs. This, in turn, swells the compulsion that results in a downward spiral of addiction.

Seniors can expect to be less able to fight all diseases (and alcoholism *is* a disease) as they grow older. For example, the liver, the organ that has the job of oxydizing alcohol, exerts a slower (often 50 percent slower) activity the longer an elderly person drinks. Since a young person's body requires one hour to process each ounce of alcohol, it is obvious that an older body will permit several ounces of alcohol to have almost unlimited time to attack the organs of the body before being oxydized—and there isn't any cell that cannot be damaged by alcohol. Also, body cells become weaker, less stable and more overworked as longevity continues. So alcohol has an unimpeded destructive course through vital organs for those who continue to drink heavily as they grow older.

Adding insult to aging, alcohol creates an accumulation of damage to vital organs, which actually accelerates the process of aging. The older drinker looks older and feels older than he or she really is. It is one of the pleasant surprises of recovery when men and women of all ages start looking younger.

Most older alcoholics, noting their conditions in a mirror, rush to buy and gulp down handfuls of vitamins. It is a losing cause. Few ever learn that alcohol is a retardant to the helpfulness of all vitamins and minerals. No matter how much an elderly drinker's body needs nutrients, alcohol makes them useless.

The alcohol we drink speeds up the urinary loss of all soluable nutrients. Researchers have stated that between thirty and forty of the most needed nutrients to maintain good health are rendered useless to the body by alcohol. Alcohol also causes the accumulation of blood fat to double.

These facts may never impress stubbornly denying elderly alcoholics who are sure none of this (if they ever read or hear) applies to them. But it still may alert family members who live in fear of serious illnesses for those they love and who may bear the burden of caring for the ill drinker.

When friends and relatives of a senior alcoholic face the reality that alcohol certainly makes older drinkers so unsteady that they are likely to fall and break bones, friends and family may become seriously involved in caring for the older person. There is also the often-occurring tragedy when an elderly drinker who also smokes passes out while holding a cigarette and suffers serious or fatal burns.

The journey to alcoholism is also accelerated for senior drinkers by the fact that they may be popping pills while they drink. Most of these tablets and capsules are "downers" such as barbiturates, tranquilizers and painkillers.

Today, users of soporifics, which are in the same ether-family as alcohol, find a notation on the container supplied by the druggist that states "No Alcohol." Most often, older users fail to read or merely shrug off the warning with, "That doesn't apply to me."

What the pill-popping drinker doesn't know is that the combination of the pill drug and the liquid drug does not simply double the potency of the dose but quadruples the power.

Seniors frequently are already overmedicated when they begin increasing their intake of alcohol. It is estimated that citizens over sixty-five years of age make up 10 percent of this country's population—and that 10 percent ingests 25 percent of all prescribed drugs.

But correctly regulating the supply of sleeping pills and painkillers to seniors is hard to accomplish. They may go to several physicians at the same time. They know they can get the needed prescription from several doctors without any of them knowing that they are double-dealing—perhaps triple-dealing.

This may be an appropriate time to mention that the big hidden problem of alcoholism and drug abuse among seniors sometimes starts with the incautious prescribing practices of doctors. Statistics report that every month there are more than six million appointments with physicians kept by senior citizens. Medical specialists may be prescribing pills and medicine to an individual without knowledge that others are also prescribing. Even a friendly nurse, a dentist or a therapist can add to the supply of pills.

When an elderly "pill popper" is an alcoholic, he or she is on treacherous ground. Alcoholics are notoriously excessive. Their thinking is, "If one pill is good for me, four will really work miracles." Hence, they overmedicate while they overdrink.

Any potential elderly alcoholic is likely to be plied with advice to take a nip at night to sleep better, another before dinner to whet the appetite, another after meals to aid digestion and still more whenever jittery nerves need calming. In many retirement homes, cocktail hours are conducted every afternoon for conviviality. Some elderly patrons are benefitted. But there always are secret problem drinkers who find these occasions to be "recommended" excuses to overdrink.

Added to the older alcoholic's excessiveness is the inevitable forgetfulness of the elderly. A natural lapse of memory is abetted by the dulling of memory by alcohol. When oldsters can't recall if they took that "regular dosage," they want to make sure it is taken, so they often down a second dose.

As a depressant, alcohol is an ultra-attractive drug for seniors. Since alcohol anesthetizes the brain and other organs of the body, the elderly drinker values its ability to ease aches and pains. Actually, alcohol only makes the drinker *unaware* of pain. The hurting, as well as its source, goes merrily along under the wraps of the sedation and may later return in fuller force. For example, a stomach ulcer's pain is dulled, but the incessant penetration of tissue by acids created by alcohol goes on and worsens the original condition.

Another vicious cycle emerges. The more alcohol relieves pain, the more the desire for that "wonder liquid" grows. And the more alcoholism speeds up its progression. An addiction is developed. And addiction always is a disease process rather than a symptom of something else. Addiction feeds on itself.

So easily does the emotional affect the physical.

Society prompts the elderly, rich in experience, to be fearful of failure. When they lose power over alcohol, they think negatively, lose self-esteem and confidence, feel inadequate in everything and avoid facing problems. The realization of an involvement with booze sharpens a sense of guilt. In turn, the bottle tells them, "It's okay. I'm your comfort." But anxiety, temporarily suppressed by alcohol, will thrive anew later—even stronger. And so the importance of sedation grows.

8

The Promises
of Recovery

There is, indeed, no generation gap in alcoholism. Not in the road drinkers take to acquire the addiction. Nor in the path that both young and old travel toward a stable and rewarding recovery in hospital units and treatment facilities dedicated to sobriety. And not in the miraculous return to reality found in the program which is practiced by all those in the fellowship of Alcoholics Anonymous.

Within those programs, the older alcoholic is guided toward finding himself or herself again. The revelations will be surprising, sometimes astounding, always gratefully accepted. Many seniors have discovered truth in the "Big Book," *Alcoholics Anonymous*, that reports, "The age of miracles is still with us. Our own recovery proves that."

And we seniors also find guidance in such quotes from the book as "We feel that a man is unthinking when he says that sobriety is enough" and most asssuredly in two other "surprises."

One resides in the shortest paragraph in the book: "It works—it really does." The other precious words are, "We will find lifetime friends."

Seniors are often surprised that they are grateful not just for sobriety but for having fallen victim to a disease which, had it never been our lot to have, would never have given an older drinker a reason to experience the joys of life before death in A.A. and to learn to love the men and women who they would never have met had they not become alcoholic.

A.A. also allows us to be honest about denial.

It is natural for older drinkers to deny a problem with alcohol. Experiences during a long life may well lead an aged man or woman to minimize the threat from sipping too much from a bottle, *especially* if the problem has not become truly acute until the later years. Why should one who has lived through gigantic challenges fear a substance that brought earlier joys and eased pain?

We should again consider the fact that the stigma of being considered a "common drunk" militates against an elderly person's conceding a drinking problem. All stigmas (divorce, bankruptcy, a "wayward" son or daughter, etc.) affect senior citizens—so why not feel we are looked down on because we "sometimes drink too much"?

The fact is, we senior citizen boozers sincerely believe what we deny. The older drinker mistrusts younger persons, especially a "nosy" recovering alcoholic. And perish the thought of a grandchild pleading "Quit drinking, Grandpa." The befuddled mind of the aged alcoholic despises "whipper-snapper brats who cause all society's troubles."

Yet, on November 22, 1969, I listened to my daughter, who took me to my first Alcoholics Anonymous meeting where I met and related to a roomful of youths. I have never had a drink since that evening. And a seventeen-year-old granddaughter began giving me "birthday" cakes to celebrate my sobriety anniversary.

She has continued the practice and now works the steps as an active member of Overeaters Anonymous.

One end result of the stubborn nonacceptance of us older drinkers is a compounding of rejections, failures, feelings of inadequacy and sensitivity to any display of disgust by others. This brings about a self-pitying defeatist attitude. At an age when a man or woman ought to "have their head on straight" (as a result of a lifetime of experience), the alcoholic's mind is so confused, realistic thinking is usually next to impossible.

In recovery, an oldster finds that while there are few variations in symptoms and recovery techniques between age brackets, there are differences in attitudes. Many of us who are retired on pensions or disability have lost a meaningful role in life. Not so with ambitious youths or the working, family-raising, security-seeking middle-aged citizens. When boredom, loneliness and a sense of no longer being needed by society creeps into the consciousness of the senior citizen, a great emotional void exists. The most readily available and surest "filler" is the bottle.

So we elderly imbibers do not begin drinking to intoxication primarily to experience fun, an emotional high, or a party-lover's thrill, which is sometimes why younger people first begin drinking heavily. Oldsters almost always drink to escape from a problem, usually a physical one. Alcohol helps one forget pains and troubles. For an oldster liquor is a panacea, a reliable painkiller.

Elderly drinkers are often driven by depression. Their drinking is a gesture of defeat. Such elders have little to live for. They believe they might as well be drunk as where they are.

In recovery, we seniors can again explore the subject of stress, an enemy of everybody's good health. For the elderly, it can be a subtle slayer. An older drinker is often subjected daily to trying to cope with aspects out of a society which they are unlikely to understand because they matured in a world where living was simpler.

All authorities in the field of alcoholism agree that few chemicals imbibed by mankind are more conducive to an aftermath of stress than alcohol. The drug (no matter what form is ingested) always produces a temporary sedative effect, followed by an agitation which persists in cultivating jitters, sweats and stress.

Not only does stress prove more devastating to the body and emotions of us seniors (often nurturing the suicidal urge) but it has the little-known capability of deteriorizing, year by year, the immune system—the safeguard old bodies need to ward off illnesses.

The longer stress is experienced and the older the stressed person is, the more damage is done to the body's ability to guard against disease. And, sadly, this can serve to accelerate aging. The end result is increased chances of all addictions—including alcoholism.

At any time, an oldster can recall how often lecturers, magazine and newspaper articles, books and TV documentaries still flood aging men and women with advice on how to live longer and feel younger. We are truthfully told we need not act or think old. We need only to keep as active as we can, eat properly, think positively and stay alert to life's possibilities. Adherence to these simple and effective health rules, however, can never work when one is killing pain or time by imbibing alcohol.

Social interests and involvements have long kept seniors concerned with the young side of themselves. Yet a heavy drinker sinks into isolation and loneliness with only one companion—the bottle.

And, of all the great assurances to the elderly, the one promise rarely, if ever, enjoyed by old drinkers is that sexual activity promotes healthy, cheerful senior years.

"You are not too old to have satisfying sex," authorities tell the elderly. But mankind has known for centuries that alcohol reduces sexual capabilities, even promoting impotency. What can elderly alcoholics think of themselves when this promise rarely is fulfilled, and never wholly?

We older alcoholics often bemoan life's unkept promises. A recovery program, if honestly worked on every day, *will* keep its promises. What are these promises? You'll feel better, you'll receive love and give love in return, and you'll learn to be the best "you" possible in the years that remain ahead.

9
Old Drinkers Can Change

The all-too-erroneous image persists of an old soak who is a grizzled, whiskered, toothless, ragged, begrimed man, sucking on a wine bottle. Or a "fallen" female passed out in a flophouse or beer joint.

One of the tragedies of society's misunderstanding of alcoholism is that people cannot accept an average, well-groomed old tippler as a real drunk, yet can see the disease, often with amusement, in a colorful writer, actor, playboy or executive or an affluent social lioness with a snootful.

People are guilty of spreading false conceptions when they say that an elderly male drinker "is not the type," or a grande dame "doesn't fit the image."

More tragic by far, however, is the attitude of others that it is "too late and hopeless" for older alcoholics to recover. People are released from involvement in a senior citizen's booze problem when their attitude is, "It's too late," "She's too old to change her habits," "It's a hopeless task," "They're too stubborn and selfish to listen," or "He'll die soon no matter what we do."

Every known fact points to the reality that old people *can* change. There's no such thing as helpless and hopeless. Old dogs *can* learn new tricks. Any alcoholic hurts many other people besides him- or herself. No one is too old to quit. It's not too late to find a new life and begin a new era of character growth.

But alcohol is such an incubator for inconsistent and knee-jerk thinking by the problem drinker that concerned relatives and friends are frequently in a "damned if I do and damned if I don't" situation. Looking away from a problem often tells a senior citizen with a distorted and drunken perspective who may be ready to accept help that, "They don't really care; they'd prefer that I die." Many have become discouraged from admitting their problem by interpreting other people's embarrassment as disinterest.

The neglect senior citizen alcoholics may see or feel often is real and of their own doing. Stubborn refusal to cooperate is discouraging to would-be helpers.

A common remark from relatives and friends is, "She keeps complaining about pain." Of course oldsters suffer. They add the pain of alcohol withdrawals to the simple act of living in a world full of stress and discomfort. Alcohol makes the pain of living worse, not better. Another typical comment is, "All he has to do is stop drinking the stuff, so why doesn't he?" Alcoholism is a disease. The alcoholic cannot stop through will power alone. He or she needs help to stop.

Senior citizen alcoholics have a threefold problem: they have a physical disease (alcoholism), they have the "insanity" of alcoholic thinking and they have all the attendant difficulties that naturally come with growing older.

Elderly drinkers are trying to live in a youth-oriented society. Americans for generations have coveted young appearances and young activities. The search for the fountain of youth is universal. The accent now is more pronounced than ever.

Women get the barrage heavily. Magazine and TV ads constantly urge them to reject the "golden years." Beauty aids abound. Dieting and magic potions and pills are in vogue. Men are also targets of the "Don't look your age" advice.

Returning to youth is made to seem so easy. When oldsters naturally fall short of what they are told is possible, they experience a sense of rejection that leads to drinking for comfort.

Yet, closer to home, the elderly encounter family and friends who feel like protecting them "from themselves." They hear: "You're too old to do that kind of thing," "Act your age, Pops," "There's no fool like an old fool."

Even small chores and activities long enjoyed are called off-limits by well-intentioned others. Elders are told to leave those things to younger, more eager, more steady hands.

What else besides sit and sip can Grandpa do when he constantly hears, "You have to take care of yourself . . . don't have a heart attack . . . you'll hurt yourself doing things like that."

One of the ironies of aging is that senior citizens may turn to the same kind of copy-cat behavior that youths exert in smoking, drinking, gambling like Mom and Dad. A retiree who envies the energy of youths will see no reason why he can't match the fun drinking of the young. The young seem so capable of "holding it." Why, reasons the oldster, can't my longer life and vast experience let me top that guzzling brat?

Sadly, and all too often, some relatives or friends go too far in the attempt to shield senior citizens from the negative side of growing older. They are doing the elderly no favors in refusing to let them be exposed to facts about alcoholism in old age because "it might depress the poor souls."

In fact, experts in aging have said that the two greatest fears of people in retirement are obesity and alcoholism. And many social drinkers quickly become excessive users *after* retirement. Some men and women have been teetotalers or social drinkers until they have retired.

Despite encouragement to "make the second half the better half," the elders often feel they have been "discarded." The wisdom of old age prompts those detached from the work force to reason correctly that society has betrayed them by failing, or refusing, to make use of the excellent talents and skills arising out of experience. Small wonder that they are sad and sometimes bitter.

Most wage-earners are required to be people-pleasers to some extent. After a lifetime of currying the favor of bosses or customers, retirees find they can be their own person. They are no longer answerable for how they spend their time. Drinking to one's heart's content is a form of independence. A retiree who has experienced busy forty-hour weeks for decades may long for challenges. Alcohol seems to fill the void.

Feel sorry for the big executive after he ceases being a big wheel? The "time on his hands" he experiences is comparable to the futility felt by the senior citizen woman. She used to nurture young lives and run a household sometimes combining a career with motherhood. She could bake, sew, can fruits and vegetables or make jellies. Now a retired businesswoman or housewife finds the easiest time-filling chore is to tipple.

Especially conducive to heavy drinking is the attitude of those who are victims to forced retirement. Their life expectancy averages only another five to ten years. Their suicide rate increases twelvefold after forced retirement. A third of their marriages fail. A proper mood arises for heavy drinking.

Societal prejudices and bleak economic circumstances force elderly drinkers into seclusion. What a blessing they consider their isolation.

When an older person feels bored, lonely and useless to society, he or she needs a one-to-one friendship. The bottle often fills that need and can be enjoyed behind closed doors.

Loneliness breeds the "thinking that leads to drinking."

It is not only those drinking senior citizens living on small fixed incomes or even below the poverty level who go into hiding to drink. It happens to many affluent or "comfortable means" elders. Surveys of excessive drinking by oldsters in expensive "retirement villages," where only well-fixed citizens can live, reveal this fact.

Older alcoholics usually prefer privacy in drinking. They patronize stores that deliver for convenience. They have community trash bins for anonymous stashing of empties. They are treated by home-call doctors. Their apparent well-cared-for status curtails snooping by relatives who otherwise might worry about "how Aunt Millie is doing."

In one village of seniors, a resident guessed that one-half had drinking problems. In another senior city, an estimated three thousand elderly alcoholics patronized the top-grossing liquor store in the state. A survey in another "home" for the elderly showed a peak in incidences of alcoholism in the sixty-five to seventy-four group.

So hidden are these elderly exiles that not even family members suspect the extent of any individual's drinking until a fall or physical collapse causes hospitalization. Even then, these oldsters can con relatives and wind up being "revolving door" patients for detoxification.

Senior citizen alcoholics are hidden because unenlightened citizens refuse to believe there really could be any drinking problem among the elderly. "Alcoholics always wind up in drunk tanks," "Imagine Grandma driving drunk," and "Gramps wouldn't hurt a fly," are typical attitudes.

Close friends and family, even doctors, mistake unsteadiness, confusion and mumbling speech as senility. Seniors are slower, more undecided, tardy in reflexes, even walk unsteadily. But the blanket term, "senility," is now recognized as inaccurate. There are a number of diseases which cause the symptoms once generally attributed to simply being old. Senility does not automatically accompany old age.

But old alcoholics are artful in pretending to be senile or have physical ailments to cover drunkenness. Even spouses buy the deceit.

Realities escape many when it comes to believing an elderly person can be an alcoholic. Many an adult son or daughter has happily mixed a "toddy" for an alcoholic father or mother believing that "It'll do him (or her) good. It's just what the doctor ordered." How unwittingly and tragically can one become an enabler. Relatives of a drunken mother or father will refuse to admit, even face the possibility, that a parent is in the grip of alcohol. Public knowledge of that would be a family disgrace.

For the "comfortably-fixed" elderly, affluence can be a tragedy. A small percentage of senior citizens, but still large enough to cause concern, face their final years with sizable incomes. Many of them, alas, die "graciously" from alcoholism. They imbibe the costliest liquors, believing that dipsomania comes only from cheap booze, never the fine "drinks" of connoisseurs. Some can afford private nurses, chauffeurs, long stays in elaborate detoxification clinics. They are truly hidden from all but themselves and their trusted servants. It is unthinkable to society that they can be alcoholics.

So, elderly alcoholics have many reasons to start drinking, and they keep on drinking for many reasons, enabled by the disbelief or disinterest of their families and friends. Yet, none of this changes the fact that they *can* stop drinking. At any age, if we want something enough and if we're given the information and the moral support, we can change. Every happy, sober member of Alcoholics Anonymous is testament to this truth.

"It's too late" is only true when you allow it to be. Why not adopt another motto: Better late than never.

10

Toward Solutions

The words of advice most useful in pointing a senior citizen alcoholic toward sobriety are not separate ideas but are intertwined. They are:

1. Admit and accept the disease.
2. Identify and relate to peers.
3. Know that somebody really cares.

So long as denial and antagonism exist in older drinkers, there can be no start at recovery. Elderly alcoholics must face reality. They have to be aware that nobody can do it for them but they also cannot do it alone. Older alcoholics must know that nobody is too old to reach for sobriety and that it never is too late or too hopeless to make the reach.

The no-generation-gap credo must prevail. Elderly drinkers are basically no different in their alcoholic drinking and recovery program than alcoholics of any age. Nor does alcoholism play favorites. While each person travels their own special road to chronic drunkenness, once they are there they behave and think like those of any other race, creed, age or social status.

Elderly alcoholics entering upon a recovery program have better chances personally if they engage in "rap" sessions with their peers and discuss problems of aging as those problems relate to problem drinking. But the goals are the same for the young as for senior citizens.

Although discussion in any group is a vital part of recovery, elders are more comfortable, and hence motivated toward sobriety more quickly if in contact with peers. Oldsters do have peculiarities due to less tolerance to loud noises from "babes in arms." They have diminished eyesight and hearing ability. Some find difficulty in breathing in smoke-filled rooms. Large crowds can cause intimacy to be lost. Experts usually recommend small groups for newly sober elders.

The first persons to start the process toward sobriety for drinking grandparents are those closest to the older alcoholic. They do, however, usually face the most resistance and likelihood of failure. They may be able merely to point the way to the well-traveled road to recovery. But even that is valuable. Loved ones must be properly aware of how and where to point. They are usually the most instrumental in bringing about a caring intervention by trained professionals.

Retirement robs elders of one of the most effective sobriety-achievers in operation—the big stick of employers. Industrial programs for alcoholic employees have the best recovery record today, often from 65 to 85 percent of all workers who are advised to recognize their problem and encouraged to participate in company-sponsored programs. A younger worker gets nudged into dealing with his or her problem. But a drunken employee of sixty-three or sixty-four is often forced into early retirement or is fired.

Remember that the elderly's constant cry is "nobody cares." Any indication of caring by others can diminish denial to some extent.

Any volunteer at a local Alcoholics Anonymous service center or intergroup can corroborate the fact that many middle-aged sons and daughters call to ask how a parent's drinking can be halted. Even calls come from grandchildren, pleading, "Please help my grandmother. I love her so much." All too often, old drinkers refuse to believe any progeny of theirs cares a damn. Even more often, family or friends who have reason to suspect a problem in an older person know little about the complexities of alcoholism and behavior of alcoholics.

The reasons why there are experts in the field of alcoholism, especially in hospitals and treatment facilities, is that it is so easy for a layman to say the wrong or ill-advised thing to a problem drinker of any age.

In order to take a first step *with* a drinking senior citizen, a person close to the alcoholic must equip himself with some knowledge of the disease. Even a "crash" course can create helpful understanding.

Nobody can be forced into sobriety. The alcoholic must, on his or her own, ask for help. For example, Alcoholics Anonymous will advise someone who telephones, "Your mother must call us herself." A caller may be directed to Al-Anon for families of alcoholics, or Alateen for youths growing up with a drinking parent or grandparent, or Adult Children of Alcoholics. These programs are designed to help the nonalcoholic live his or her own life.

Obviously, for best results, a sick elderly alcoholic should become a patient in a hospital with special programs for problem drinkers. There are many in successful operation today. Information about these facilities can generally be obtained from a local Alcoholism Council. An oldster can undergo detoxification and treatment as a start toward sobriety through abstinence.

Assurance that the older drinker can stay with recovery is found in hospitals and treatment centers because they have follow-up programs after a patient is released. The "rap sessions" among peers during treatment are continued for alumni. This is vital for oldsters, since patients over sixty-five often may not be admitted to halfway houses where younger ages find help.

All those fine plans for luring an older alcoholic into a hospital, however, won't work unless they go willingly. Forced confinement is not only impractical, but often doomed to failure. Most alcoholic wards readily inform patients and family that people cannot be helped against their will. Even if they could be, the antagonism created in an elderly drinker by unwelcomed confinement may persist for the remainder of a painful lifetime. It is futile to tell them, "It's for your own good."

It is true, of course, that A.A. is full of good members who first came, resentfully, to that fellowship through orders from the court. They obeyed to save a driver's license or escape jail. And some of them got the "message" and stayed on—sober. Many, unfortunately, do not care to "keep coming back" after the number of required meetings are completed.

So it is of primary importance for a willingness, an open-mindedness—a *want-to-get-sober* wish—to accompany the senior citizen alcoholic to those doctors, nurses, therapists, counselors and treatment facilities. Is this impossible? Decades ago, only miracles accomplished that. Now there are new approaches.

In the early days of A.A., members, needing other alcoholics on whom to work in order to strengthen their own sobriety, dragged drunks out of bars and smothered them with attention. A limited lasting success resulted. Four years after A.A. was founded, there were only one hundred sober members nationwide.

Failures spurred the long-accepted belief that alcoholics had to hit bottom—emotionally, physically and/or financially—before being approached. A.A. still insists on the alcoholic personally asking for help before he can be started on the road of recovery.

If a problem drinker will not listen even after hitting bottom, he will be unable to accept aid. But there always remains the possibility that an older drinker *can* be "led to water" by the use of intervention which has been alluded to previously.

Meanwhile, nonalcoholics need to become well versed in alcoholic behavior and symptoms. If they cannot go to "understanding alcoholism" classes, they can talk with personnel at alcoholism councils or read books. Many of these become involved in meaningful volunteerism that brings untold rewards in personal satisfaction. And rewards for the older alcoholic who regains sobriety. By becoming well informed, when the alcoholic asks for help, or just indicates that he or she is fed up with living alcoholically, the nonalcoholic can perhaps provide alternatives without putting the alcoholic on the defensive.

The chains of alcoholism grow so gently that they often are felt only when they are of nearly unbreakable strength.

Elderly alcoholics must realize that they have become captives against their will, regardless of how strong their guilt and shame.

They can well pity those who heap stigma on all old drunks once they have escaped from addiction. Nonalcoholics can never, never know the sheer joy of those men and women who have broken those chains of bondage and emerged into a bright new world where they once more have the opportunity to grow emotionally and spiritually. Recovering elderly alcoholics are lucky that the ability to learn and to improve will never leave them.

With gratitude at being permitted a return to life, the recovering senior citizen drinker comes to consider himself or herself the luckiest person alive—if the drinker takes advantage of the opportunity to grow and reap the rewards of sobriety.

With the alcohol-induced cobwebs out of mind, the recovering senior citizen finds that there is still *life before death*. They have added years to their lives and life to their years.

Old people CAN change. Many in their sixties and seventies are going back to college or night classes, starting new activities at senior citizen centers, volunteering to help those who are less fortunate.

Senility, or fear of it, fades with sobriety. Researchers have learned that the body may change but the mind is ageless. "Aging is a necessity, but maturity is a choice." Recovering alcoholics learn to choose. They want to open new avenues of knowledge.

By choice, the recovering elderly alcoholic wants to return to a world where he is not considered different from other humans.

A slowdown in response to stimuli has nothing to do with mental ability. In fact, while the elderly learn, more slowly than the young, they comprehend just as well and their decisions are likely to be more correct.

Sober elders are not washed up mentally. With restored good health and habits, seniors find that their minds have now become more, not less, facile with age. So it's difficult to drive at night. That's a relatively small thing compared to the many blessings to think about.

Recovering old drunks learn to look for interesting positives instead of carping negatively about natural handicaps. Such people learn the trick of compensation—substituting new and desirable interests for outmoded things lost.

During recovery programs with peers, seniors become involved and stay involved. That keeps them happy. The correlation between happiness and activity is higher for persons in the seventies than those in the fifty to sixty groups. Such elders are not satisfied with going through the motions at anything. "Doing" is fulfilling.

The tools oldsters are given for overcoming the addiction to alcohol can be used in sober living. These recovering drunks, almost unwittingly, become better family members and public citizens in their later years. These tools include: humility, gratitude, serenity, being a good listener, having a well-developed spiritual side.

Helpful in the growth of senior citizens after recovering from alcoholism is the practice taught them of being unconcerned about the past. If they are trained not to look back at irreparable actions, they live well today and dream well tomorrow.

How wrong we are when we say, "Why not let them go out drinking? They've got so little time left at best."

One recovering alcoholic who sobered at the age of seventy recently said in his eightieth year: "I have grown more in the past ten years than in any part of the previous seventy years due to what I have learned on the process of getting and staying sober."

Physically, alcoholism is a primary disease. Before any of the ailments that result from alcoholism can be cured, alcoholism must be arrested. Abstinence must be achieved. The same principle of recovery applies to all of the hoped-for psychological benefits of sobriety. They cannot be attained until character defects caused by "stinking thinking" are cleared up.

Therefore, I as an older alcoholic who put the cork in the bottle more than nineteen years ago, had to clear away emotional wreckage before I could strive for the finer emotions of life. All of us oldsters must learn to cope (knowing we'll never be wholly rid of any of them) with our character defects.

"Special interest" groups are not encouraged among Alcoholics Anonymous members as the *only* sharing experiences for those who are learning to grow spiritually in the program. But some segments of recovering alcoholics like to augment general meetings of all kinds with gatherings where men and women who share specific interests can give and receive.

When I walked into a young people's meeting of A.A. in 1969, there were no meetings where most of those attending were senior citizens. Also no pamphlets aimed at older drinkers. Now there are both senior meetings and literature in which elderly drinkers share their stories.

The first A.A. groups for seniors began in 1978 in southern California. Now an older newcomer (or long-timer) can exchange thoughts weekly with men and women of their own general age (as well as younger members who often pay visits—since all A.A. groups are open to members of all ages).

In my area, four different locations offer regular meetings for older alcoholics. "Nobody cares" is not a valid excuse to allow drinking to make the later years a living death.

Sobriety for the senior alcoholic is indeed a matter of losses and gains. Those that are lost include loneliness, boredom, a feeling of uselessness, self pity, feelings of inadequacy and a fear of the unknown.

In return, the sober oldster counts among his or her gains: an alert mind, character growth, a purpose for living, the meaning of caring and sharing, a motivation to live and a solid maturity.